DICTIONARY OF ARTIFICIAL INTELLIGENCE AND ROBOTICS

BY THE SAME AUTHOR

Automation, Manpower, and Education

The Computer Prophets

The Death of Privacy: Do Industrial and Government Computers Threaten Our Personal Freedom?

Dictionary of Business and Management, 2nd edition

Inside the Wall Street Journal: The History and Power of Dow Jones & Company and America's Most Influential Newspaper

Dictionary of Banking and Financial Services, 2nd edition

Dictionary of Computers, Data Processing, and Telecommunications

The Investor's Dictionary

DICTIONARY OF ARTIFICIAL INTELLIGENCE AND ROBOTICS

Jerry M. Rosenberg, Ph.D.
Professor, Graduate School of Management
Chairman, Department of Business Administration
Faculty of Arts and Sciences
Rutgers University
Newark, New Jersey

JOHN WILEY & SONS
New York · Chichester · Brisbane · Toronto · Singapore

Library of Congress Cataloging-in-Publication Data:
Rosenberg, Jerry Martin.
  Dictionary of artificial intelligence and robotics.

  Bibliography: p.
  1. Artificial intelligence—Dictionaries. 2. Robotics
—Dictionaries. I. Title.

Q334.6.R67 1986   629.8′92   86-15975
ISBN 0-471-84982-0
ISBN 0-471-84981-2 (pbk.)

Printed in the United States of America

10 9 8 7 6 5 4 3 2 1

**to
the memory of
my parents,
Esther and Frank**

PREFACE

Significant interest and research in artificial intelligence and robotics began only 20 years ago but in this short time span an entirely new vocabulary has been born. The major objective of artificial intelligence is to make machines smarter. Secondary goals include understanding what intelligence is and making devices more useful.

Robots are leading the way in our new industrial revolution, increasingly carrying out the work of people. These robots are advanced automation systems that utilize computers as an integral part of their functioning. Joined together by computer-controlled technology, artificial intelligence and robotics represent the most exciting new scientific and commercial enterprises for the remainder of this century.

This work of more than 4000 terms has been prepared with the hope that awareness of the accepted meanings of terms may enhance the process of sharing ideas. Though it cannot eliminate the need for the user to determine how a writer or speaker treats a word, this dictionary shows what usages exist. It should reduce arguments about words and assist in stabilizing terminology. Most important, it should aid people in speaking and writing with greater clarity.

A word can take on different meanings in different contexts. There may be as many meanings as there are areas of specialization. A goal of this dictionary is to be broad and to establish core definitions that represent the variety of individual meanings. My purpose is to enhance parsimony and clarity in the exchange process within the fields of artificial intelligence and robotics.

Many terms are used in different ways. I have tried to unite them without the bias of giving one dominance over another. Whenever possible (without creating a controversy), I have stated the connection among multiple usages. Commonly used symbols, acronyms, and abbreviations are also given.

Most dictionaries that deal with similar subjects tend to define their task rather narrowly, whereas this work purports to identify individual specialties and then proceeds to specify the relationships among robotics, artificial intelligence, and computer-control terms useful in developing appropriate software programs.

Organization

This is a defining work rather than a compilation of facts. The line is not easy to draw because in the final analysis meanings are based on facts. Consequently, factual information is used where necessary to make a term more easily understood. All terms are presented in the language of those who use them. Obviously, the level of complexity needed will vary with the user—one person's complex definition is another's precise and pithy statement. Several meanings are sometimes given; the relatively simple for the layperson, the more developed and technical for the specialist.

I have organized this dictionary to provide information easily and rapidly. Keeping in mind two categories of users—the experienced person who demands precise information about a particular word and the newcomer, support member, teacher, or student who seeks general explanations—I have in most cases supplied both general and specialized entries. This combination of umbrella entries and more technical definitions should make this dictionary an unusually useful reference source.

Alphabetization. Words are presented alphabetically. Compound terms are placed where the reader is most likely to look for them. They are entered under their most distinctive component, usually nouns, which tend to be more distinctive than adjectives. Should you fail to locate a word where you initially look for it, turn to a variant spelling, a synonym, or different words of the compound term. Entries containing mutual concepts are usually grouped for comparison. They are then given in inverted order; that is, the expected order of words is reversed to allow the major word of the phrase to appear at the beginning of the term. These entries precede those that are given in the expected order. The terms are alphabetized up to the first comma and then by words following the comma, thus establishing clusters of related terms.

Headings. The current popular term is usually given as the principal entry, with other terms cross referenced to it. Some terms have been included for historical significance, even though they are not presently in common usage.

Cross Reference. The rule followed for cross references calls for going from the general to the specific. Occasionally, "see" or "see also" references from the specific to the general are used to inform the user of words related to particular entries. "See" or "see also" references to presently accepted terminology are made wherever possible. The use of "cf." suggests words to be compared with the original entry. "Deprecated term" or "slang" indicates that the term should not be used and that there is a preferred word or phrase.

Synonyms. The words "synonymous with" or "synonym for" following a definition does not imply that the term is exactly equivalent to the principal entry under which it appears. Usually the term only approximates the primary sense of the original entry.

Disciplines. Many words are given multiple definitions based on their utilization in various fields of activity. In these cases, the definition with the widest application is given first, with the remaining definitions listed by area of specialty (identified in boldface italic type). Since the areas may overlap, the reader should examine all definitions of a term.

Feedback

The definitions given here have been reviewed by appropriate specialists and educators. However, I am solely responsible for choosing the terms to be included. The vast range of material makes it inevitable that definitions may vary based on perspective, background, and connotation. I welcome critical comments bringing errors to my attention, to make it possible to correct them in later editions, thus evolving a greater conformity of meaning for all.

JERRY M. ROSENBERG, PH.D.

New York
September 1986

ACKNOWLEDGMENTS

No dictionary can be the exclusive product of one person's effort. Even when written by one individual, such a work requires the tapping of many sources, which is especially true of this book. By the very nature of the fields included, I have had to rely on the able and extensive efforts of others.

At no time have I deliberately quoted a definition from another copyrighted source. Any apparent similarity to existing, unreleased definitions is purely accidental and the result of the limitations of language. Much assistance has come indirectly from books, journal articles, and reference materials. They are too numerous to be named here. Various organizations have aided me directly by providing informative source materials, and some government agencies and not-for-profit associations have provided a considerable amount of usable information, as well.

On a more personal level, I thank the various individuals whom I used as a sounding board to clarify my ideas and approach; they offered valuable suggestions and encouraged me to go on with the project. Stephen Kippur, executive publisher, and Nettie Bleich, my editor, both of John Wiley & Sons, had the foresight to initiate this book, and with sensitivity and creativity followed it through to publication. I also thank my wife, Ellen and my daughters, Lauren and Elizabeth, who continue, after five dictionaries, 2,500 pages and more than 50,000 defined terms, to show understanding, and who offered full support during the preparation of this dictionary.

J.M.R.

A

A: see *analog.*

ABEL: an experimental medical system for diagnosing acid/base electrolyte disorders.

abort: to cease a process immediately.

abort branch: a special software routine, included in the controls for stationary baseline tracking robots, that constantly monitors the position of the tracking window. If, at any time during automatic operation, the robot's TCP coordinate in the tracking direction coincides with the coordinate of either limit of the tracking window, the robot control immediately initiates an abort branch that will direct the robot to exit from the part along a pretaught safe path relative to the part.

absolute address

(1) an address in a computer language that identifies a storage location or a device without the use of any intermediate reference.

(2) an address that is permanently assigned by the machine designer to a storage location.

(3) synonymous with *explicit address, machine address, specific address.*

absolute order: in computer graphics, the display command in a computer program that causes the display units to interpret the data bytes following the order as absolute data rather than as relative data.

AC: see *acoustic coupler.*

ACC: see *accumulator.*

acceleration time: that part of access time required to bring an auxiliary storage device, typically a tape drive, to the speed at which data can be read or written.

access: the manner in which files or data sets are referred to by the computer.

access-oriented method: a programming method based on the utilization of probes that trigger new computations when data are changed or read.

access time

(1)   the time interval between the instant at which an instruction control unit initiates a call for data and the instant at which delivery of the data is completed. Access time equals latency plus transfer time.

(2)   the time interval between the instant at which data are requested to be stored and the instant at which storage is started.

(3)   the deprecated term for *cycle time.*

ACCUM: see *accumulator.*

accumulator (ACC) (ACCUM)

(1)   a device in which the result of an arithmetic or logical operation is determined.

(2)   a register that stores a quantity. When a second quantity is entered, it arithmetically combines the quantity and stores the result in the location of the register.

accuracy

(1)   a quality held by that which is free of error.

(2)   a qualitative assessment of freedom from error, a high assessment corresponding to a small error.

(3)   a measure of the magnitude of error, preferably expressed as a function of the relative error, a high value of this measure corresponding to a small error.

(4)   the difference between the actual position response and target position wanted or commanded of an automatic control system. cf *precision.*

acid/base electrolyte disorder: see *ABEL.*

ACK (acknowledge)

(1)   affirmative acknowledgment; used in block transmission, indicates that the previous transmission block was accepted by the receiver and that it is ready to accept the next block of the transmission.

(2)   the communication by the addressee of a message informing the originator of a communication that a message was received and understood.

acknowledge character

(1)   a transmission control character transmitted by a station as an affirmative response to the station with which the connection has been set up.

(2) a transmission control character transmitted by a receiver as an affirmative response to a sender. An acknowledge character may also be used as an accuracy control character.

acoustic coupler (AC): a type of telecommunication equipment that permits use of a telephone network for data transmission by means of sound transducers.

action: in a production system with a forward-chaining architecture, the right-hand side of a rule consists of a sequence of actions, each of which performs an activity such as creating, deleting, or modifying elements in data memory, performing input/output, modifying production memory, and halting the recognize-act cycle. When a rule fires, the actions that constitute the right-hand side are performed in sequence, utilizing the bindings that were formed when the rule was instantiated.

activation: an associated number representing the degree to which that object receives attention. Activations are propagated between related objects in a network. see also *activation cycle, activation network.*

activation cycle: the period of time during which activation is propagated among adjacent objects. During each such cycle activation is propagated one arc farther from the source of activation, with one or more activation cycles taking place during a single recognize-act cycle.

activation network: a graph, each node of which represents an object, with each arc representing a relationship between two objects. Should the arc be labeled, the label is a number showing the strength of the relationship.

active accommodation: the integration of sensors, control, and robot motion allowing alternation of a robot's preprogrammed motions in response to felt forces. This approach stops a robot when forces attain set levels or perform force feedback tasks like insertions, door opening, and edge tracing.

active illumination: illumination that is varied automatically for extracting more visual information from a scene (e.g., by switching lights on and off, adjusting brightness, altering the color of the illumination).

active value: a special value that can be altered in the course of a consultation; used with graphic images to permit the user to alter the value in a system by simply altering an image on the computer screen.

actuating signal: an input impulse in the control circuitry of computers.

actuator: a motor; a transducer for converting electrical, hydraulic, or pneumatic energy to impact on the motion of a robot.

3

A/D: see *analog-to-digital converter.*

ADA: a high-level language for real time processing problems. Developed in 1983 by computer scientists at New York University, it is the first successful version of a key program for the U.S. Department of Defense to develop a standard computer language for the military. It is named after Augusta Ada Byron, Lord Byron's daughter, who is considered the world's first computer programmer.

adaptable

(1) *general:* multipurpose; able to be redirected, retrained, or utilized for new tasks.

(2) *robotics:* the reprogrammability or multitask capability of robots. Capable of making self-directed corrections with the aid of visual, force, or tactile sensors.

adaptive control: a control technique where control parameters are continuously and automatically adjusted in response to measured process variables in order to achieve near optimum performance.

adaptive robot: an intelligent robot that automatically adjusts its task to changing environmental condition, relying heavily on sensors and artificial intelligence to determine its motions.

ADCCP: Advanced Data Communication Control Procedures. An American National Standards Institute protocol for communication.

addend: in an addition operation, a number or quantity added to the augend.

adder (ADDR)

(1) a device whose output data are a representation of the sum of the numbers represented by its input data.

(2) a device whose output is a representation of the sum of the quantities represented by its inputs.

ADDR: see *adder.*

address (ADRS)

(1) a character or group of characters that identifies a register, a particular part of storage, or some other data source or destination.

(2) to refer to a device or an item of data by its address.

(3) that part of the selection signals that indicates the destination of a call.

addressability

(1) in micrographics, the number of addressable positions within a

specified film frame, as follows: number of addressable horizontal positions multiplied by number of addressable vertical positions.

(2) in graphics, the number of addressable points within a specified display space or image space.

address format

(1) the arrangement of the address parts of an instruction.

(2) the arrangement of the parts of a single address such as those required for identifying a channel, module, or track on magnetic disk.

address modification

(1) any arithmetic, logic, or syntactic operation performed on an address.

(2) altering the address part of a machine instruction by means of coded instruction.

address register: a register in which an address is stored.

adjacency: in character recognition, a condition in which the character spacing reference lines of two consecutively printed characters on the same line are separated by less than a specified distance.

ADP: see *automatic data processing.*

ADRS: see *address.*

Advanced Data Communication Control Procedures: see *ADCCP.*

advanced memory allocation: in a computer language, space in memory allocated for variables in the program before the program is executed.

advice taking: synonymous with *learning from instructions.*

advisory system: an expert system that interacts with a person in the style of giving advice rather than in the style of dictating commands; possesses mechanisms for explaining its advice and for permitting users to interact at a detail level comfortable to the user.

affirmative acknowledgment: see *ACK.*

agenda: an ordered list of actions. Some knowledge systems store and reason about possible actions; for example, whether to pursue a specific line of reasoning. HEARSAY uses agenda-based control.

AI: see *artificial intelligence.*

AL: see *assembly language.* see also *AML.*

algebraic language: an algorithmic language, many of whose statements are structured to resemble the structure of algebraic expressions, for example, ALGOL and FORTRAN.

ALGOL (algorithmic language): a language primarily used to express computer programs by algorithms; requires compiler translation.

algorithm: a finite set of well-defined rules for the solution of a problem in a finite number of steps; for example, a full statement of an arithmetic procedure for evaluating sin X to a stated precision. cf. *heuristic.*

algorithmic language: see *ALGOL.*

alphabet

(1) an ordered set of all the letters used in a language, including letters with diacritical signs where appropriate, but not including punctuation marks.

(2) an ordered set of symbols used in a language; for example, the Morse code alphabet.

alphabetic character: a letter or other symbol (excluding digits) used in a language.

alphabetic character set: a character set that contains letters and may contain control characters, special characters, and the space character, but not digits.

alphabetic character subset: a character subset that contains letters and may contain control characters, special characters, and the space character, but not digits.

alphabetic string

(1) a string consisting solely of letters from the same alphabet.

(2) a character string consisting solely of letters and associated special characters from the same alphabet.

alphameric: synonymous with *alphanumeric.*

ALPHANUM: see *alphanumeric.*

alphanumeric (ALPHANUM): pertaining to a character set that contains letters, digits, and usually other characters such as punctuation marks. synonymous with *alphameric.*

alphanumerical code: a code according to which data is represented using an alphanumeric character set.

alphanumeric character set: a character set that contains both letters and digits and may contain control characters, special characters, and the space character.

alphanumeric character subset: a character subset that contains both letters and digits and may contain control characters, special characters, and the space character.

ALV: see *arithmetic logic unit.*

6

American National Standards Institute (ANSI): an organization for the purpose of establishing voluntary industry standards.

American Standard Code for Information Interchange: see *ASCII.*

AML: A Manufacturing Language. A robotics language for programming robots developed by IBM. see also *assembly language.*

analog (A): pertaining to data in the form of continuously variable physical quantities.

analog communications: the transfer of information via a continuously variable quantity such as the voltage produced by a strain gauge or air pressure in a pneumatic line.

analog computer
(1) a computer in which analog representation of data is mainly used.
(2) a computer that operates on analog data by performing physical processes on these data. cf. *digital computer.*

analog control: control by communication signals that are physically or geometrically isometric to the variables that are being controlled, usually by a person. Any unit for effecting such control. cf. *symbolic control.*

analogical control: robot control that uses communication signals which are isomorphic to the variables being controlled by a human operator.

analogical inference: mapping information from a known object or process description into a less-known, but similar one.

analogical means-ends analysis: a problem-solving technique where a new problem is solved by transforming the solution of a similar older problem into a solution for the new problem utilizing operators that reduce differences between corresponding solution descriptions. see *analogical problem space; means-ends analysis.*

analogical problem space: a problem space whose states are descriptions of problem solutions, and whose operators transform one specific problem solution into a closely related one. see also *analogical means-ends analysis.*

analog-to-digital converter (A/D)
(1) a functional unit that converts analog signals to digital data.
(2) a device that senses an analogical signal and converts it to a proportional representation in digital form.
(3) an electromechanical device that senses an electrical signal and converts it to a proportional representation in digital form.

analog transmission: transmission of a continuously variable signal as opposed to a discrete signal. Physical quantities such as temperature

7

are described as analog while data characters are coded in discrete pulses and referred to as digital.

AND: a logic operator having the property that if *P* is a statement, *Q* is a statement, *R* is a statement, . . . then the AND of *P*, *Q*, *R*, . . . is true if all statements are true, false if any statement is false. synonymous with *logical multiply*.

and node: see *and/or tree.*

AND operation: synonymous with *conjunction.*

and/or tree: a proof tree in theorem proving and a goal tree in general problem solving in which each node is labeled as either an *and* node or an *or* node. For *and* nodes, each of the child nodes indicates needed subproofs or subgoals that must be achieved jointly if the parent node is to be achieved. For *or* nodes, each of the child nodes specifies a sufficient alternative subproof or subgoal, only one of which need be achieved if the parent node is to be achieved. see also *goal tree.*

android: a robot approximating a person in physical appearance.

annunciator: a visual or audible signaling device, operated by relays, that indicates conditions of associated circuits designed to attract attention.

ANSI: see *American National Standards Institute.*

antecedent: the statement of the conditions needed for drawing a conclusion. In a production system, the left-hand side of the rule encodes the antecedent conditions for the rule to fire, while the right-hand side encodes the consequent conditions.

anthropomorphic: humanlike or able to duplicate human traits.

aperture

(1)   one or more adjacent characters in a mask that cause retention of the corresponding characters.

(2)   an opening in a data medium or device such as a card or magnetic core; for example, the aperture card combining a microfilm with a punched card, or a multiple aperture core.

(3)   a part of a mask that permits retention of corresponding portions of data.

APL (A Programming Language)

(1)   a language with an unusual syntax and character set, primarily designed for mathematical applications, particularly those involving numeric-on-literal arrays.

(2)   a general purpose language for diverse applications such as com-

mercial data processing, system design, mathematical and scientific computation, data base applications, and mathematical instruction.

application: in software, a program that aids an individual to perform a practical task.

application-oriented language: synonymous with *problem-oriented language.*

applicative language: a programming language in which computations are expressed as nested function calls rather than sequences of statements (e.g., LISP).

APT: Automatically Programmed Tool. A high-level or simplified programming language.

arbitrary sequence computer: a computer in which each instrument explicitly determines the location of the next instruction to be executed.

architecture
(1) a specification which determines how something is constructed, defining functional modularity as well as the protocols and interfaces which allow communication and cooperation among modules.
(2) the physical and logical structure of a computer or manufacturing process.

arithmetic logic unit (ALU): the element able to perform basic data manipulations in the central processor; usually, the unit can add, subtract, complement, negate, rotate, AND, and OR.

arithmetic overflow: synonymous with *overflow.*

arithmetic register: a register that holds the operands or the results of operations such as arithmetic operations, logic operations, and shifts.

arithmetic shift: a shift, applied to the representation of a number in a fixed-radix numeration system and in a fixed-point representation system, in which only the characters representing the absolute value of the number are moved. An arithmetic shift is usually equivalent to multiplying the number by a positive or a negative integral power of the radix except for the effect of any rounding.

arm: an interconnected set of links and powered joints operating as a manipulator, and supporting or moving a hand or end effector.

array
(1) an arrangement of elements in one or more dimensions.
(2) in assembler programming, a series of one or more values represented by a fixed symbol.

(3)   in FORTRAN, an ordered set of data items identified by a single name.

(4)   in PL/1, a named, ordered collection or data elements, all of which have identical attributes. An array has dimensions specified by the dimension attribute, and its individual elements are referred to by subscripts. An array can also be an ordered collection of identical structures.

(5)   in APL, BASIC, and RPGII, a systematic arrangement of elements in a table format.

articulated arm: an artificial jointed arm able to duplicate some of the motions of a human arm.

artificial intelligence (AI):   the capability of a device to perform functions that are normally associated with human intelligence such as reasoning, learning, and self-improvement.

artificial vision: a branch of artificial intelligence where engineers develop software for letting devices recognize shapes and respond differentially, based on the perceived shapes. Robots and some military weapons utilize artificial vision for detecting entities.

ARU: see *audio response unit.*

ASCII: American Standard Code for Information Interchange. The standard code, using a coded character set consisting of seven-bit coded characters (eight bits including parity check), used for information interchange among data processing systems, data communication systems, and associated equipment. The ASCII set consists of control characters and graphic characters.

ASM: see *assembler.*

assemble

(1)   to translate a program expressed in an assembly language into a computer language, and perhaps to link subroutines. Assembling is usually accomplished by substituting the computer language operation code for the assembly language operation code and by substituting absolute addresses, immediate addresses, relocatable addresses, or virtual addresses for symbolic addresses.

(2)   to prepare a machine language program from a symbolic language program by substituting absolute operation codes for symbolic operation codes and absolute or relocatable addresses for symbolic addresses.

assembler (ASM):   a software program for translating assembly language instructions into machine language form; translates symbolic codes into machine language and assigns memory locations for variables and constants. synonymous with *assembly program.*

assembly language (AL): a source language that includes symbolic machine language statements in which there is a one-to-one correspondence with the instruction and data formats of the computer.

assembly program: synonymous with *assembler.*

assembly robot: a programmed, designed, or specialized robot that places parts together into subassemblies or total products.

associative storage: a storage device whose storage locations are identified by their contents, or by part of their contents, rather than by their names or positions. synonymous with *content-addressed storage.*

assumption
(1) a plausible statement within a theory that has not been verified.
(2) a self-evident definition in which truth is accepted within the system.

asynchronous computer: a computer in which each event or the performance of each operation starts as a result of a signal generated by the completion of the previous events or operation, or on the availability of the parts of the computer required by the next event or operation. cf. *synchronous computer.*

asynchronous operation
(1) an operation that occurs without a regular or predictable time relationship to a specified event; for example, the calling of an error diagnostic routine that may receive control at any time during the execution of a computer program.
(2) a sequence of operations in which operations are executed out of time coincidence with any event. synonymous with *asynchronous working.*

asynchronous processing: processing in which each step is dependent on the completion of the previous step.

asynchronous working: synonymous with *asynchronous operation.*

atom: in LISP, a fundamental, singular element that cannot be decomposed; for example, in the list "3 blind mice," 3, blind, and mice are atoms; unit entities that cannot be divided into other related structures.

attribute: the property of an object; for example, net worth as an attribute of a loan applicant. Attributes are associated with values in specific cases. see also *descriptor.*

audio-response: a form of output that uses verbal replies to inquiries.

11

The computer is programmed to seek answers to inquiries made on a time-shared, on-line system, and then to utilize a special audio response unit which elicits the appropriate prerecorded response to the inquiry.

audio response unit (ARU):   an output device that provides a spoken response to digital inquiries from a telephone or other device. The response is composed from a prerecorded vocabulary of words and can be transmitted over telecommunication lines to the location from which the inquiry originated.

augend: in an addition operation, a number or quantity to which numbers or quantities are added.

automated office: a workplace that utilizes computers and robot devices to do office work.

Automatically Programmed Tool: see *APT.*

automatic data processing (ADP)
(1)   data processing performed by computer systems.
(2)   data processing largely performed by automatic means.
(3)   the branch of science and technology concerned with methods and techniques relating to data processing, largely performed by automatic means.

automatic programming: the process of using a computer to perform some stages of the work involved in preparing a program.

automation
(1)   the implementation of processes by automatic means.
(2)   the conversion of a procedure, process, or equipment to automatic operation.
(3)   the theory, art, or technique of making a process more automatic.
(4)   the investigation, design, development, and application of methods of rendering processes automatic, self-moving, or self-controlling.

automaton: an automatic device that continually repeats tasks.

autonomy: a system's capability to interact independently and effectively with its environment via its own senses and actions. Robotics represents ultimate computer autonomy.

auxiliary memory: the storage area supplementary to the main memory. Slower than main memory, no manipulation of data can take place in the auxiliary mode. cf. *main memory.*

auxiliary operation: an off-line operation performed by equipment not under control of the processing unit.

axes: directions of movement based on a coordinate system.

azimuth: the direction of a straight line to a point in a horizontal plane; expressed as the angular distance from a reference line such as the observer's line of view.

B

B: see *binary.*

back chaining: see *backward chaining.*

background processing: the execution of lower priority computer programs when higher priority programs are not using the system resources.
cf. *foreground processing.*

backlash: the free play in a gear system in terms of link motion.

backtracking: the method of backing up through a sequence of inferences, often in preparation for trying a different path. Planning problems
usually require backtracking approaches that permit a system to try one
plan after another as unacceptable outcomes are identified.

Backus-Naur Form (BNF): a formal language expressing context-free
grammars. The grammar consists of a set of rewrite rules, each of which
has a left-hand side and a right-hand side, separated by the metalanguage symbol :: = .

backward chaining: one of several control methods for regulating the
order in which inferences are drawn. In a rule-based system, backward
chaining is initiated by a goal rule. The system attempts to determine if
the goal rule is correct. It backs up to the *if* clauses of the rule and tries
to determine if they are correct. This, in turn, leads the system to consider other rules that might confirm the *if* clauses. In this way, the
system backs into its rules. Eventually, the back-chaining sequence
ends when a question is asked or a previously stored result is found.
synonymous with *model-directed.*

balanced merge: an external sort that places strings created by an
internal sort phase on half of the available storage devices and then
merges strings by moving them back and forth between an equal number of devices until the merging process is complete.

band

(1)   a group of tracks on a magnetic drum or on one side of a magnetic
disk.

15

(2) in data communication, the frequency spectrum between two defined limits.

bandwidth: the maximum number of data units that can be transferred along a channel per second.

bang-bang control: control accomplished by a command to an actuator that at any time informs it to operate either in one direction or the other with maximum energy. cf. *bang-bang-off control.*

bang-bang-off control: control accomplished by a command to an actuator that at any time informs it to operate either in one direction or the other with maximum energy, or to do nothing. cf. *bang-bang control.*

bang-bang robot: synonymous with *pick-and-place robot.*

base

(1) *robotics:* the platform or structure to which a robot arm is attached; the end of a kinematic chain of arm links and joints opposite to that which grasps or processes external objects.

(2) *computer control:* a number that is multiplied by itself as many times as indicated by an exponent.

base address

(1) a numerical value that is used as a reference in the calculation of addresses in the execution of a computer program.

(2) a given address from which an absolute address is derived by combination with a relative address.

base number: a quantity that specifies a system of representation for numbers.

BASIC: Beginner's All-Purpose Symbolic Instruction Code. A programming language with a small repertoire of commands and a simple syntax, primarily designed for numerical application. With BASIC, program statements can be written in any order because each statement is given a number for identification purposes.

basic resolution unit: see *BRU.*

batch manufacture: the production of parts in discrete runs or batches, interspersed with other production outputs or runs of other parts.

baud

(1) a unit of signaling speed equal to the number of discrete conditions or signal events per second. For example, one baud equals one half dot cycle per second in Morse code, one bit per second in a train of binary

signals, and one three-bit value per second in a train of signals, each of which can assume one of eight different states.

(2) a unit of digital signaling rate. The signaling rate in bauds is equal to the reciprocal of the length in seconds of the signal element when all signal elements have equal lengths.

(3) in asynchronous transmission, the unit of modulation rate corresponding to one unit interval per second; that is, if the duration of the unit interval is 20 milliseconds, the modulation rate is 50 baud.

BCD: see *binary coded decimal notation.*

Beginner's All-Purpose Symbolic Instruction Code: see *BASIC.*

BEL character (BEL): a control character that is used when there is a need to call for human attention and which may activate an alarm or other attention devices.

belief

(1) a hypothesis.

(2) an accepted confidence in a specific orientation.

bilateral manipulator: a master/slave manipulator with symmetric force reflection having both master and slave arms with sensors and actuators, so that in any degree of freedom a positional error between the master and slave leads to equal and opposing forces applied to the master and slave arms.

BIN: see *binary.*

binary (B) (BIN)

(1) pertaining to a selection, choice, or condition that has two possible values or states.

(2) pertaining to a fixed-radix numeration system having a radix of two.

binary arithmetic operation: an arithmetic operation in which the operands and the result are represented in the pure binary numeration system. synonymous with *dyadic operation.*

binary boolean operation: synonymous with *dyadic boolean operation.*

binary chop: synonymous with *binary search.*

binary code: a code that makes use of only two distinct characters, usually 0 and 1.

binary coded decimal code: synonymous with *binary coded decimal notation.*

binary coded decimal (BCD) notation: a binary coded notation in which each of the decimal digits is represented by a binary numeral; for example, in a binary coded decimal notation that uses the weights 8-4-2-1, the number "23" is represented by 00100011 (compare its representation 10111 in the pure binary numeration system). synonymous with *binary coded decimal code; binary coded decimal representation; coded decimal notation.*

binary coded decimal representation: synonymous with *binary coded decimal notation.*

binary coded notation: a binary system in which each of the decimal digits is represented by a binary numeral.

binary data: data written in binary, octal, or hexadecimal forms which can indicate various codes used for computer operations.

binary digit: synonymous with *bit.*

binary element: a constituent element of data that takes either of two values or states. The term bit, which is the original abbreviation for the term binary digit, is misused in the sense of binary element or in the sense of Shannon.

binary image: a black-and-white image represented in memory as zeros and ones. Images appear as silhouettes on the video display monitor.

binary notation

(1) any notation that uses two different characters, usually the binary digits 0 and 1; for example, the gray code. The gray code is a binary notation, but not a pure binary numeration system.

(2) fixed-radix notation where the radix is two. For example, in binary notation the numerical 110.01 represents the number 1×2 to the first power plus 1×2 to the minus 2 power; that is, $6\frac{1}{4}$.

(3) a binary number. Loosely, a binary numeral.

binary number: a component of computer language that usually contains more than one figure. The digits used are 0 and 1.

binary numeral: a numeral in the pure binary numeration system; for example, the binary numeral 101 is equivalent to the Roman numeral V.

binary numeration system: synonymous with *pure binary numeration system.*

binary operator: synonymous with *dyadic operator.*

binary picture: a digitized image where the brightness of the pixels can have only two values such as white or black or zero or one.

binary program space (BPS): a segment of a computer's memory, just above the LISP microkernel, containing compiled codes for functions and programs utilized during execution of LISP programs; overlaps the heap to include the static heap.

binary search: a dichotomizing search in which, at each step of the search, the set of items is partitioned into two equal parts, some appropriate action being taken in the case of an odd number of items. synonymous with *binary chop.* see also *dichotomizing search.*

Binary Synchronous Communication Protocol: see *BISYNC.*

binding: an association between a variable and a value for that variable that holds within some scope such as the scope of a rule, function call, or procedure invocation.

biped: two legged. cf. *octopod.*

bipolar logic: synonymous with *transistor-transistor logic.*

biquinary code: a notation in which a decimal digit n is represented by a pair of numerals, a being 0 or 1, b being 0, 1, 2, 3, or 4, and $(5a + b)$ being equal to n. The two digits are often represented by a series of two binary numerals.

bistable: that which is able to assume one of two stable states; a flip-flop circuit is bistable.

BISYNC: Binary Synchronous Communication Protocol. An early standard protocol half-duplex communication developed about 1965.

bit

(1) in the pure binary numeration system, either of the digits 0 and 1. synonymous with *binary digit.*

(2) the smallest possible unit of information. One bit is enough to tell the difference between two opposites such as yes or no.

bit-map display: a display composed of a large array of small, individually controllable dots. Advanced types have a million or more dots, each of which may be more or less bright, or in color.

bit string: a string consisting solely of bits.

blackboard: see *blackboard architecture.*

blackboard architecture: an expert system design in which several independent knowledge bases examine a common working memory, called a *blackboard.* An agenda-based control system continually examines all of the possible pending actions and selects the one to try next. synonymous with *HEARSAY architecture.*

blackboard model: the model of a reasoning process in which different parts of the system communicate with each other through the intermediary of a structure called *blackboard.* see also *blackboard architecture.*

19

blank column detection: the collator function of checking for and signaling error conditions should a blank column be found in a specific data field.

BLK: see *block.*

blob: any group of connected pixels in a binary image.

block (BLK)

(1) a string of records, a string of words, or a character string formed for technical or logic reasons to be treated as an entity.

(2) a set of things (e.g., words, characters, or digits) handled as a unit.

(3) a collection of contiguous records recorded as a unit. Blocks are separated by interblock gaps and each block may contain one or more records.

(4) a group of bits, or *n*-ary digits, transmitted as a unit. An encoding procedure is generally applied to the group of bits or *n*-ary digits for error control purposes.

block diagram: a diagram of a system, a computer, or a device in which the principal parts are represented by suitably annotated geometrical figures to show both the basic functions of the parts and their functional relationships.

block sort: a sort that separates a file into segments (using the highest-order portion of the key), orders the segments separately, and then joins them.

BNF: see *Backus-Naur Form.*

BOOL: see *boolean.*

boolean (BOOL)

(1) pertaining to the processes used in the algebra formulated by George Boole.

(2) a value of 0 or 1 represented internally in binary notation.

boolean ADD: synonymous with *OR.*

boolean algebra: a mathematical system relating logical functions instead of numbers. Boolean operatives such as "AND," "OR," and "NOR" are used to compare one expression to another. In computers, logical operations utilizing boolean algebra result in conditions serving as input into branching functions in the programs.

boolean function: a switching function in which the number of possible values of the function and each of its independent variables is two.

Boot: see *bootstrap.*

20

bootstrap (BOOT)

(1)   an existing version, perhaps a primitive version, of a computer program that is used to establish another version of the program.

(2)   a technique or device designed to bring itself into a desired state by means of its own action; for example, a machine routine whose first few instructions are sufficient to bring the rest of itself into the computer from an input device.

(3)   that part of a computer program used to establish another version of the computer program. cf. *initial program loader.*

BORIS: an experimental, narrative-understanding natural language system.

borrow digit: a digit that is generated when a difference in a digit place is arithmetically negative and that is transferred for processing elsewhere. In a positional representation system, a borrow digit is transferred to the digit place with the next higher weight for processing them.

bound: a variable assigned a value by the process of binding; said to be bound to that value.

BPS: see *binary program space.*

branch

(1)   a set of instructions that is executed between two successive branch instructions. see also *branching.*

(2)   in the execution of a computer program, to select one from a number of alternative sets of instructions.

(3)   the means of departing from the sequence of the main program to another routine or sequence of operations as shown by a branch instruction whose execution is dependent on the conditions of the results of computer operations. synonymous with *jump.*

branching: a computer operation, like switching, where a selection is made between two or more possible courses of action, depending on some related fact or condition. A robot must possess the ability to execute conditional branches in order to react intelligently to its environment. The wider the variety of tests it is able to perform, the better it can react. see *conditional branching; offset branching; standard branching.*

branch instruction: an instruction that controls branching. synonymous with *decision instruction.*

breadboard: an experimental model of a unit used to test the parameters of the design; usually a circuit board that has a specific configuration on it.

breadth-first search: in a hierarchy of rules or objects, refers to a technique in which all of the rules or objects on the same level of the hierarchy are examined before any of the rules or objects below them are checked.

breakaway force: the resistive force such as static friction that is not constant as the relative velocity increases.

break package: a mechanism in a programming or knowledge engineering language for telling the program where to stop so that the programmer can examine the values of variables at that point.

breakpoint

(1) a place in a computer program, usually specified by an instruction, where its execution may be interrupted by external intervention or by a monitor program.

(2) an instruction address stop that can be established by command.

broadband: synonymous with *wide band.*

BRU: basic resolution unit. The smallest incremental change in axial position that the feedback unit can sense. Usually equal to the smallest allowable position increment in robot task programming.

bubble sort: an exchange sort in which the sequence of examination of pairs of items is reversed whenever an exchange is made. synonymous with *sifting sort.*

buffer storage: a storage device that is used to compensate for differences in the rate of flow of data between components of an automatic data processing system, or for the time of occurrence of events in the components.

bug: any mistake in a computer program.

bulk storage: synonymous with *mass storage.*

bulk transfer units: see *transfer units.*

burst

(1) in data communication, a sequence of signals counted as one unit in accordance with some specific criterion or measure.

(2) to separate continuous-form paper into discrete sheets.

bus

(1) one or more conductors used for transmitting signals or power.

(2) an information coding scheme by which different signals are coded and identified when sharing a common data channel.

byte

(1) usually, 8 bits of information.

(2) a binary character operated on as a unit and usually shorter than a computer word.

(3) the representation of a character.

C

C: a low-level, efficient, general purpose programming language associated with the UNIX operating system; usually used for system programming.

cable drive: a robotic system where the power is transmitted from an actuator to a remote mechanism by using cables and pulleys.

caching: storing an answer to a frequently occurring question (problem) to avoid a replication of past efforts. see *rote learning*.

CAD: see *computer-aided design*.

CAD/CAM: computer-aided design/computer-aided manufacturing. A parts design and manufacturing method utilizing a computer data base where drawings are not needed. synonymous with *computer-integrated manufacturing (CIM)*.

CADUCEUS: a diagnosis system for internal medicine. Previously called *INTERNIST*.

CAI: see *computer-aided instruction*.

calculus: in artificial intelligence, a calculus of something is a method of analyzing, using special symbols.

calibration
(1) determining, marking, or rectifying the capacity or scale gradations of a measuring instrument or replicating unit.
(2) determining the deviation from standard so as to ascertain the proper correction factors.

CALISTO: an experimental system for modeling and monitoring large projects.

call
(1) the action of bringing a computer program, a routine, or a subroutine into effect, usually by specifying the entry conditions and jumping to an entry point.
(2) in computer programming, to execute a call.

25

(3)   a transmission for the purpose of indentifying the transmitting station for which the transmission is intended.

(4)   an attempt to reach a user, whether or not successful.

(5)   to transfer control to a specified closed subroutine.

(6)   synonymous with *cue.*

calling a function: synonymous with *function call.*

CAM: see *computer-aided manufacture.*

CAM-I: Computer-Aided Manufacturing-International, Inc. Provides a convenient conduit for transferring information between firms using computers in design and manufacturing, and users and vendors of numerical control equipment and robot systems.

canned explanations

(1)   *software:*   a fixed, displayed message explaining an action taken by a computer system.

(2)   *expert systems:*   explains solutions to problems; they are not efficient since a programmer must anticipate each conceivable explanation for every conceivable solution.

card code: the combinations of punched holes that represent characters (e.g., letters, digits) in a punched card.

card field: a specific combination of punch positions, mark-sensing positions, or both, on a card.

carry (CY)

(1)   the action of transferring a carry digit.

(2)   one or more digits, produced in connection with an arithmetic operation on one digit place of two or more numerals in positional notation that are forwarded to another digit place for processing there.

(3)   the number represented by the digit or digits in (2).

(4)   the command directing that a carry be forwarded.

(5)   to transfer a carry digit.

carry bit: a conditional status flat bit contained in a CPU accumulator.

carry digit: a digit that is generated when a sum or a product in a digit place exceeds the largest number that can be represented in that digit place and which is transferred for processing elsewhere. In a positional representation system, a carry digit is transferred to the digit place with the next higher weight for processing there.

Cartesian coordinate robot: a robot whose manipulator is degrees of freedom as defined primarily by Cartesian coordinates.

Cartesian coordinate system: a coordinate system whose axes or dimensions are three intersecting perpendicular straight lines and whose origin is the intersection. synonymous with *rectangular coordinate system.*

CASNET: casual-associative network. An experimental system for dealing with disease processes; associated with a specific application focusing on glaucoma.

casual-associative network: see *CASNET.*

cathode-ray tube (CRT): a vacuum tube display in which a beam of electrons can be controlled to form alphanumeric characters or symbols on a luminescent screen; for example, by use of a dot matrix. synonymous with *video display terminal.*

causal analysis: used in credit (blame) assignment to track the probable causes of observed events. see also *credit (blame) assignment.*

causal model: a model where the causal relations among various actions and events are represented explicitly.

CCD camera: a solid-state camera using a charge-coupled device (CCD) for transforming a light image into a digitized image. A CCD camera is similar to a CID camera, except that its method of operation forces readout of pixel brightnesses in a regular line-by-line scan pattern. There is only one readout station, and charges are shifted along until they reach it. cf. *CID camera.*

CCP: see *communication control program.*

CCU: see *central control unit.*

cell: a manufacturing unit composed of a number of work stations, and the materials, transport mechanisms, and storage buffers that interconnect them.

cell control: a module in the control hierarchy for controlling a cell. The cell control module is controlled by a center control module, if one exists. Otherwise, it is controlled by a factory control level.

center: a manufacturing unit composed of a number of cells, and the materials, transport, and storage buffers that interconnect them.

center control: control decisions for two or more control tasks at different locations made at a centralized location. synonymous with *centralized control.*

center of acceleration: the point in a rigid body around which the entire mass revolves.

center of gravity: the point in a rigid body where the entire mass of the body is concentrated and produces the same gravity resultant as that for the body itself.

central control unit (CCU): the communication controller hardware unit that contains the circuits and data flow paths needed to execute instructions and to control its storage and the attached adapters.

centralized control: control decisions for two or more control tasks at different locations made at a centralized location. synonymous with *center control.*

Central Office Maintenance Printout Analysis and Suggestion System: see *COMPASS.*

central processing unit (CPU): a unit of a computer that includes circuits controlling the interpretation and execution of instructions. synonymous with *central processor; main frame.*

central processor: synonymous with *central processing unit.*

certainty: the degree of confidence one has in a fact or relationship. As used in AI, contrasts with probability, which is the likelihood that an event will occur. see *probability.*

certainty factor: a numerical weight given to a fact or relationship indicating the confidence one has in the fact or relationship. These numbers behave differently than probability coefficients. In general, methods for manipulating certainty factors are more informal than approaches to combining probabilities. Most rule-based systems use certainty factors rather than probabilities. synonymous with *confidence factor.*

CG: see *computer graphics.*

CH: see *channel.*

chad: synonymous with *chip.*

chain drive: the transmission of power from an actuator to a remote mechanism by mating tooth sprocket wheels with an adaptable chain.

chain printer: an impact printer in which the type slugs are carried by the links of a revolving chain.

channel (CH) (CHNL)

(1) in information theory, that part of a communication system that connects the message source with the message sink. Mathematically, this part can be characterized by the set of conditional probabilities of occurrence of all the possible messages received at the message sink when a given message emanates from the message source.

(2) a path along which signals can be sent; for example, data channel, output channel.

(3)   the portion of a storage medium that is accessible to a given reading or writing station; for example, track, band.

(4)   in data communications, a means of one-way transmission.

CHAR: see *character.*

character (CHAR) (CHR)

(1)   a member of an agreed-on set of elements that is used for the organization, control, or representation of data. Characters may be letters, digits, punctuation marks, or other symbols, often represented in the form of a spatial arrangement of adjacent or connected strokes or in the form of other physical conditions in data media.

(2)   a letter, number, punctuation mark, or special graphic used for the production of text.

(3)   a letter, digit, or other symbol that is used as part of the organization, control, or representation of data. A character is often in the form of a spatial arrangement of adjacent or connected strokes.

character recognition

(1)   the identification of characters by automatic means.

(2)   the identification of geographic, phonic, or other characters by various means including magnetic, optical, or mechanical.

character set

(1)   a finite, agreed-on set of different characters that is considered complete for some purpose.

(2)   a set of unique representations called characters; for example, the 26 letters of the English alphabet, 0 and 1 of the boolean alphabet, the set of signals in the Morse code alphabet, and the 128 ASCII characters.

character subset: a selection of characters from a character set, comprising all characters that have a specified common feature; for example, in each of the character sets of the International Standards Organization (ISO) Recommendation R646 (6- and 7-bit coded character sets for information processing interchange), the digits 0 and 9 may constitute a character subset.

check digit

(1)   a digit used for the purpose of performing a check.

(2)   a digit of a check key.

(3)   one or more redundant digits in a character or word which depend on the remaining digits in such a way that, should a change of digits

29

occur in data transfer operations, the malfunction of equipment can be detected.

check out: synonymous with *debug.*

Chinese binary: synonymous with *column binary.*

chip

(1) in micrographics, a piece of microform that contains both micro-images and coded identification.

(2) a minute piece of semiconductive material used in the manufacture of electronic components.

(3) an integral circuit on a piece of semiconductive material.

(4) synonymous with *chad.*

CHNL: see *channel.*

CHR: see *character.*

chunk: a collection of facts stored and retrieved as a single unit. The limitations of working memory are defined in terms of the number of chunks that can be handled at the same time.

CID camera: a solid-state camera using a charge-injection imaging device (CID) for transforming a light image into a digitized image. The light image focused on the CID generates minority carriers in a silicon wafer, which are then trapped in potential wells under metallic electrodes held at an elevated voltage. In a CID camera, pixels of the image are read out in an arbitrary sequence. cf. *CCD camera.*

CIM: synonymous with *CAD/CAM.*

circuit

(1) in data communications, a means of two-way communication between two data terminal installations.

(2) a system of conductors and related electrical elements through which electrical current passes.

(3) a communication link between two or more points.

CL: see *command language.*

clear (CLR)

(1) to put one or more storage locations or registers into a prescribed state, usually that denoting zero.

(2) to cause one or more storage locations to be in a prescribed state, usually that corresponding to zero or the space character.

CLK: see *clock.*

clock (CLK)

(1) a device that measures and indicates time.

(2)   a register whose content changes at regular intervals in such a way as to measure time.

(3)   a device that generates periodic signals used for synchronization.

(4)   equipment that provides a time base used in a transmission system to control the timing of certain functions such as sampling, and to control the duration of signal elements.

closed loop: a loop that has no exit and whose execution can be interrupted only by intervention from outside the computer program in which the loop is included.

closed-loop control: control accomplished by a closed feedback loop; that is, by measuring the degree to which actual system response conforms to desired system response, and utilizing the difference to drive the system into conformance.

closed subroutine: a subroutine of which one replica suffices for the subroutine to be linked by calling sequences for use at more than one place in a computer program. cf. *open subroutine.*

closure: in LISP, when an environment is attached to a function definition.

CLR: see *clear.*

CM: see *core memory.*

CMND: see *command.*

CMOS: Complementary Metal-Oxide Semiconductor. Chips that use far less electricity than other types because their circuits are relatively immune to electrical interference and operate in a wide range of temperatures. In CMOS, transistors on the chip are paired, with one requiring positive voltage to work and the other negative. The transistors thus offset or complement each other's power requirements. see also *MOS.*

CMPM: see *computer-managed parts manufacture.*

CNC: see *computer numerical control.*

CNTL: see *control.*

CNTR: see *counter.*

CNTRL: see *control.*

COBOL

(1)   Common Business Oriented Language. A simplified programming language designed for business data processing applications.

(2)   a general purpose (machine) language designed for commercial data utilizing a standard form. It is a language that can present any

business program to any suitable computer and also act as a means of communicating these procedures among people.

code

(1)   a set of specific rules which determines the manner in which data may be represented in a discrete form. synonymous with *code; coded character set; code set; coding scheme.*

(2)   a set of items such as abbreviations that represents the members of another set.

(3)   to represent data or a computer program in a symbolic form that can be accepted by a data processor.

coded character set: synonymous with *code.*

coded decimal notation: synonymous with *binary coded decimal notation.*

codes: see *group classification codes; sequence codes; significant digit codes.*

code set: synonymous with *code.*

coding scheme: synonymous with *code.*

COLL: see *collator.*

collate: to alter the arrangement of a set of items from two or more ordered subsets to one or more other subsets each containing a number of items, commonly one, from each of the original subsets in a specified order that is not necessarily the order of any of the original subsets.

collator (COLL):   a device that collates, merges, or matches sets of punched cards or other documents.

color: in optical character recognition, the spectral appearance of the image dependent on the spectral reflectance of the image, the spectral response of the observer, and the spectral composition of incident light.

column binary: pertaining to the binary representation of data on cards in which the weights of punch positions are assigned along card columns; for example, each column in a 12 row card may be used to represent 12 consecutive bits. synonymous with *Chinese binary.* cf. *row binary.*

COM: see *computer output microfilmer.*

combinational logic element: a device having at least one output channel and zero or more input channels, all characterized by discrete states, such that at any instant the state of each output channel is completely determined by the states of the input channels at the same instant.

command (CMND)

(1)   a control signal.

(2)   loosely, a mathematical or logic operator; an instruction.

(3)   a request from a terminal for the performance of an operation or the execution of a particular program.

(4)   a character string from a source external to a system that represents a request for system action.

command language (CL):   a source language consisting primarily of procedural operators, each capable of invoking a function to be executed. synonymous with *query language; search language.*

Common Business Oriented Language: see *COBOL.*

common field: a field that can be accessed by two or more independent routines.

common language: an easily read language that is common to a group of computers and associated equipment.

common LISP: a dialect of LISP intended to serve as a standard version of LISP that can run on a number of different machines. see also *list processing.*

communication control program (CCP):   a control program that provides the services needed to operate a communication-based information processing system.

communications link: any device (usually electrical) for the transmission of information.

comparator

(1)   a functional unit that compares several items of data and indicates the result of that comparison.

(2)   a device for determining the dissimilarity of two items such as two pulse patterns or words.

COMPASS: Central Office Maintenance Printout Analysis and Suggestion System. An expert system developed to perform the analysis of maintenance messages.

compensation: logical operations found in a control scheme to counteract dynamic lags or to modify otherwise the transformation between measured signals and controller output to yield a prompt stable response.

compiled knowledge: as an individual acquires and organizes knowledge into chunks and networks, the knowledge becomes compiled. Some people compile knowledge into increasingly abstract and theoretical patterns. Others compile knowledge from practical experience. Most people begin by acquiring theoretical knowledge and then, when they finish their schooling, recompile what they have learned into practical heuristics. Expertise consists of large amounts of compiled knowledge.

compiler: a program that decodes instructions written as pseudocodes, and produces a machine language program to be executed at a later time. synonymous with *compiling program.*

compiling program: synonymous with *compiler.*

complement

(1)   in a fixed-radix numeration system, a numeral that can be derived from a given numeral by operations that include subtracting each digit of the digital representation of the given number from the corresponding digit of the digital representation of a specified number.

(2)   a number that can be derived from a specified number by subtracting it from a second specified number; for example, in radix notation, the specified number may be a given power of the radix or one less than a given power of the radix. The negative of a number is often represented by its complement.

Complementary Metal-Oxide Semiconductor: see *CMOS.*

complement-on-nine: synonymous with *nines complement.*

complement-on-one: synonymous with *ones complement.*

complete carry: in parallel addition, a procedure in which each of the carriers is immediately transferred.

complex number: a number consisting of an ordered pair of real numbers, expressible in the form $a + bi,$ where a and b are area numbers and i squared equals minus one.

composition: grouping a sequence of production rules or operators into one rule or operator. see also *production rules.*

computed path control: a control method wherein the path of the manipulator end point is computed to produce a desired result in conformance to a given criterion such as an acceleration limit or a minimum time.

computer-aided design (CAD):   a system where engineers create a design and see the proposed product in front of them on a graphics screen or in the form of computer printout.

computer-aided design/computer-aided manufacturing: see *CAD/ CAM.*

computer-aided instruction (CAI): conventional uses of computers to present instruction, either in the form of statements followed by questions, or simulations or games in which students learn to anticipate a pattern.

computer-aided manufacture (CAM): a system permitting a computer to direct the manufacture and assembly of a product.

Computer-Aided Manufacturing-International, Inc.: see *CAM-I.*

computer-assisted instruction: learning procedures utilizing computer-based teaching and testing.

computer console: a part of a computer used for communication between operator or maintenance engineer and the computer.

computer control: a computer designed so that inputs from and outputs to a process directly control the operation of elements in that process.

computer graphics (CG): methods and techniques for converting data to or from graphic display via computers.

computer-integrated manufacturing (CIM): synonymous with *computer-aided design/computer-aided manufacturing* see *CAD/CAM.*

computer language: synonymous with *machine language.*

computer-managed parts manufacture (CMPM): computer-aided manufacture of discrete parts, usually when a number of processing and product transport operations are coordinated by a computer.

computer numerical control (CNC): a state in which a number of numerical control devices are linked together via a data transmission network and brought under the control of a single numerical control machine.

computer output microfilmer (COM): a recording device that produces computer output microfilm.

computer programming: see *programming.*

computer word: a word stored in one computer location and capable of being treated as a unit. synonymous with *machine word.*

concept acquisition: see *learning from examples.*

concept attainment: see *learning from examples.*

concept description: the symbolic data structure for describing a concept, that is, to describe a class of instances in the domain under consideration. synonymous with *description; generalization.*

concept formation: see *learning from examples.*

conceptual clustering: arranging objects into classes corresponding to specific descriptive concepts instead of classes of objects that are similar according to a mathematical measure.

concurrent execution: synonymous with *multiprogramming*.

condition

(1) an antecedent.

(2) a condition element.

(3) a proposition summarizing the state of execution of a program.

conditional: only acted on when the IF condition of an IF-THEN statement is met.

conditional branching: the extension of a standard branch; the simplest way to alter a robot's path program. Limited in the sense that each branch is associated with a particular input signal to the robot control with a robot program limited to 32 standard branches.

conditional jump: a jump that takes place only when the instruction that specifies it is executed and specific conditions are satisfied.

conditional statement: a computer program direction whose execution depends on other criteria being fulfilled.

condition element: the left-hand side of a rule in a production system that is a set of patterns that is to be matched against the contents of data memory; each such pattern is referred to as a condition element. When a rule is instantiated, each condition element matches one element of data memory.

confidence factor: synonymous with *certainty factor*.

configure: to specify how the various parts of a computer system are to be arranged.

conflict resolution strategy: a particular principle applied partially to order the instantiations in the conflict set. According to this principle, each substantiation is discarded from the conflict set, precluding it from firing on that cycle.

conflict set: the set of all instantiations generated by the match process during a recognize-act cycle. The conflict resolution process chooses one instantiation from the conflict set and fires it.

conjunction: the boolean operation whose result has the boolean value 1 if and only if each operand has the boolean value 1. synonymous with *AND operation; intersection; logical product*.

CONS cell: see *CONS node*.

36

CONSIGHT: an industrial object recognition system that utilizes special lighting for producing silhouettelike images.

consistent bindings: a set of bindings of values to variables that satisfies the conditions of each pattern taken singly, and simultaneously satisfies all constraints that apply between all patterns in a set.

CONS node (cell): in LISP, a data structure containing two fields, where each field holds a pointer to another LISP data object. The data object can be an atom, another CONS node, or another LISP object. CONS nodes are highly related to LISP concepts such as dynamic memory allocation, variable binding, dynamic scoping, and garbage collecting.

CONST: see *constant.*

constant (CONST)

(1) a fixed or invariable value or data item.

(2) data with a fixed value or meaning that are available for use throughout a program.

constraint: the fact restricting the possible solutions to a problem.

consultation paradigm: patterns that describe generic types of problem-solving scenarios. Specific system building tools are usually good for one or a few consultation paradigms and not for others.

contact sensing: procedures for monitoring and converting field switch contacts into digital information for input to a computer.

contact sensor: a unit capable of sensing mechanical contact of the hand or some other part of the robot with an external object.

content-addressed storage: synonymous with *associative storage.*

context: a state in a problem-solving process. In a production system, the context is represented by a special working memory element. Usually, tasks that can be isolated are performed by production systems that are partitioned into subtasks which, originally initiated, are expected to run to completion. The rules that constitute this task each have condition elements that match the associated context element. synonymous with *task.*

context element: a working memory element that signals the state of the computation (context) and is used for purposes of control. This is an example of a control element.

context-free grammar: a grammar describing a context-free language.

context-free language: a formal language where every sentence is generated by a grammar wherein the left-hand side of each rewrite rule consists of a single nonterminal symbol.

context-parameter-value triplets: in EMYCIN, a method of representing factual knowledge. A context is an actual or conceptual entity in the domain of the consultant. Parameters are properties associated with each context. Each parameter can take on values: the parameter, age, could take the value "13 years." synonymous with *object-attribute-value triplets.*

context tree: in EMYCIN, a structured arrangement of the objects or conceptual entities that constitute the consultation domain. There may be one or more context. synonymous with *object tree.* see *EMYCIN.*

continuous-path control: methods that are divided into three basic categories based on how much information about the path is used in the motor control calculations. These are (a) the *conventional* or *servo-control approach,* which uses no information about where the path goes in the future (this is the control design used in most industrial robots and process control systems); (b) the *preview control,* synonymous with *feed-forward control,* which uses some knowledge about how the path changes immediately ahead of the robot's current location, in addition to the past and present tracking error used by the servo controller; and (c) the *path planning approach,* synonymous with the *trajectory calculation approach,* where the controller has available a complete description of the path the manipulator follows from one point to another, achieving a highly accurate coordinated movement at high speed.

continuous-path robot: a robot that functions through an infinite number of points in space, so that when joined, a smooth compound curve is created.

contouring systems: manufacturing systems with continuous-path capability.

control (CNTL) (CNTRL) (CTRL): the determination of the time and order in which the different parts of a data processing system and the devices that contain those parts perform the input, processing, storage, and output functions.

control character: a character whose occurrence in a particular context initiates, modifies, or stops a control operation. A control character may be recorded for use in a subsequent action, and it may have a graphic representation in some circumstances.

control counter: synonymous with *instruction address register.*

control element: a working memory element the sole function of which is for storing control knowledge. A context element is an example of a control element.

control hierarchy: a relationship of control elements whereby the results of higher-level control elements are used to command lower-level elements.

control key: a key on a keyboard that is held down while another key is pressed to give the other key a different function.

control knowledge: knowledge bearing on the choice of an appropriate control strategy.

controlled-path robot: a robot using a computer control system with computational potential for describing a preferred path between any preprogrammed points. The computer determines both the desired path and the acceleration, deceleration, and velocity of the robot arm along the path.

controlled path system (CPS): a method that takes advantage of the computational capability of the computer to provide the operator with coordinated control of the robot axes when teaching the unit. It also allows control of total position, velocity, and acceleration control of the robot end effector along a desired path between programmed points when in the replay or automatic mode of operation. When teaching the robot, CPS coordinates the axes in a manner that permits the operator to position and orient the end effector at desired points without having to individually command each robot axis. In addition, when teaching, the operator does not have to generate the desired path but only programs end points.

controller

(1) *general:* a device that directs the transmission of data over the data links of a network; its operation may be controlled by a program executed in a processor to which the controller is connected, or it may be controlled by a program executed within the device.

(2) *robotics:* a device that initiates and terminates the motions of a manipulator through interfaces with the manipulator's control valves and feedback devices and which can perform complex arithmetic functions to control path, speeds, and position. An interface also permits the manipulator to interact with whatever equipment is associated with the robot's task.

control (of a knowledge system): an approach used by the inference engine to regulate the order in which reasoning occurs. Backward-chaining, forward-chaining, and blackboard agendas are examples of control methods.

control program (CP): a computer program designed specifically to schedule and supervise the execution of programs of a computer system.

control strategy: a technique for choosing the next action given numerous alternative problem-solving steps.

control total: synonymous with *hash total*.

control unit (CU): a device that controls input/output operations at one or more devices. All operations are under the control of a stored program.

control word: synonymous with *key*.

conventional approach: see *continuous-path control*.

converter: a device capable of converting impulses from one mode to another such as analog to digital, or parallel to serial, or from one code to another.

convex programming: in operations research, a particular case of nonlinear programming in which the function to be maximized or minimized and the constraints are appropriately convex or concave functions of the controllable variables. cf. *dynamic programming; linear programming*.

cooperating knowledge sources: specialized modules in an expert system that independently analyze the data and communicate via a central, structured data called a *blackboard*. see *blackboard architecture*.

coordinated axis control: control wherein the axes of the robot arrive at their respective end points simultaneously, giving a smooth appearance to the motion. Consequently, the motions of the axes are such that the end point moves along a prespecified type of path (line, circle, etc.). synonymous with *end-point control*.

core memory (CM): a storage device consisting of ferromagnetic cores or an apertured ferrite plate through which sense windings and select lines are threaded.

core plane: a grid of wires on which small iron cores are strung. A series of core planes are stacked to make up main memory.

counter (CNTR) (CT) (CTR)

(1) a device whose state represents a number and that, on receipt of an appropriate signal, causes the number represented to be increased

by unity or by an arbitrary constant; the device is usually capable of bringing the number represented to a specified value; for example, zero.

(2)   a programming unit for controlling the number of times a program loop is executed.

CP: see *control program.*

CPS: see *controlled path system.*

CPU: see *central processing unit.*

credit (blame) assignment: a statement of the steps that are responsible for a success (failure) in the overall process of achievement.

cross-assembler: a program run on one computer for the purpose of translating instruction for a different computer.

cross-product: in set theory, the cross-product, or Cartesian product, of a set *A* and a set *B* is the set of all ordered pairs (*a, b*) such that *a* is a member of *A* and *b* is a member of *B.*

crosstalk

(1)   the unwanted energy transferred from one circuit, called the *disturbing circuitry,* to another circuit, called the *disturbed circuit.*

(2)   the undesired power coupled into a communications circuit from other communications circuits.

CRT: see *cathode-ray tube.*

Crysalis: an expert system for analysis of data related to protein crystallography; developed at Stanford University.

CT: see *counter.*

CTR: see *counter.*

CTRL: see *control.*

CU: see *control unit.*

cue: synonymous with *call.*

cursor

(1)   in computer graphics, a movable marker that is used to indicate a position on a display space.

(2)   a displayed symbol that acts as a marker to help the user locate a point in text, a system command, or storage.

(3)   a movable spot of light on the screen of a display device, usually indicating where the next character is to be entered, replaced, or deleted.

customizable: a computer language or other software in which a user can alter a feature and suit the feature to a specific situation; for example, LISP and most software written in LISP. Software features are fundamentally altered and may or may not run on a specific hardware installation.

CY: see *carry.*

cybernetics: the integration of systems of control and communication used in living things and applied to machines.

cyborg: a system that is part human and part machine.

cycle

(1) an interval of space or time in which one set of events or phenomena is completed.

(2) any set of operations that is repeated regularly in the same sequence. The operations may be subject to variations on each repetition.

cycle stealing: synonymous with *direct memory access.*

cycle time: see *access time.*

cylindrical coordinate robot: a robot consisting of a horizontal arm mounted on a vertical column that is capable of turning on a rotating base. The arm moves in and out while its carriage shifts up and down on a vertical unit, and both rotate together on the base.

cylindrical coordinate system: a coordinate system consisting of one angular dimension and two linear dimensions. These three coordinates specify a point on a cylinder.

D

D: see *data.*

D/A: see *digital-to-analog converter.*

DAC: see *digital-to-analog converter.*

damping

(1) a characteristic built into electrical circuits and mechanical systems to prevent unwanted oscillatory conditions.

(2) a property of a dynamic system that causes oscillations to die out and makes the response of the system approach a constant value.

DAS: see *data acquisition system.*

data (D)

(1) a representation of facts, concepts, or instructions in a formalized manner suitable for communication, interpretation, or processing by human or automatic means.

(2) any representations such as characters or analog quantities to which meaning is, or might be, assigned.

data acquisition system (DAS): a means for scanning digital and analog inputs in an order and at a rate controlled by a program. The input signals are first scaled and corrected. The resulting values can be compared against stored limits. With general purpose computation, the DAS provides an industrial control capability that can be used in process optimization and in control over complex industrial systems.

data bank

(1) a set of libraries of data.

(2) a comprehensive collection of libraries of data; for example, one line of an invoice may form an item, a complete invoice may form a record, a complete set of such records may form a file, the collection of inventory control files may form a library, and the libraries used by an organization are known as its data bank.

data base (DB)

(1) a collection of data fundamental to a system.

(2)   a collection of data fundamental to an enterprise.

(3)   a set of data that is sufficient for a given purpose or for one or several given data processing systems.

(4)   a collection of interrelated or independent data items, stored together without unnecessary redundancy, to serve one or more applications.

data base management system (DBMS):   a software system facilitating the creation and maintenance of a data base and the execution of computer programs using the data base.

data break: synonymous with *direct memory access.*

data bus: communication lines for the exchange of information.

data cell: a direct access storage volume containing strips of tape on which data are stored.

data channel (DC) (DCH):   a device that connects a processor and main storage with I/O control units. synonymous with *input/output channel.*

data code

(1)   a structured set of characters used to represent data items; for example, the codes 01, 02, . . . 12 may be used to represent the months January, February, . . . December of the data element "months of the year."

(2)   in data communications, a set of rules and conventions according to which the signals representing data should be formed, transmitted, received, and processed.

data-directed: controlled by changes in data rather than changes in objectives. cf. *goal-directed.*

data-directed inference: see *inference, data-directed.*

data driven: synonymous with *forward chaining.*

data element: a set of data items to be considered in a given situation as a unit. synonymous with *data item.*

data file: a collection of related data records organized in a specific manner; for example, a payroll file (one record for each employee, showing such information as rate of pay and deductions) or an inventory file (one record for each inventory item), showing such information as cost, selling price, and number in stock.

data filtering: limiting that part of data memory that participates in the match process to a subset for purposes of efficiency.

data flowchart: a chart that represents the path of data in the solving of a problem, and which defines the major phases of processing as well as the various data media used. synonymous with *data flow diagram.*

data flow diagram: synonymous with *data flowchart.*

data item: synonymous with *data element.*

data link (DL)

(1) the physical means of connecting one location to another for the purpose of transmitting and receiving data.

(2) the assembly of parts of two data-terminal equipments (DTEs) that is controlled by a link protocol, and that, together with the interconnecting data circuit, enable data to be transferred from a data source to a data sink.

(3) the interconnecting data circuit between two or more equipments operating in accordance with a link protocol. It does not include the data source and the data sink. see also *link.*

data memory: the global data base of a production system. The contents can be partially or totally ordered on the basis of their time of creation or most recent modification; the most volatile portion of a production system.

data object: in LISP, an object such as an atom, list, or function which itself is data in a data structure for another object.

data set: the major unit of data storage and retrieval, consisting of a collection of data in one of several prescribed arrangements, and described by control information to which the system has access.

data structure: in LISP, everything can be data that has a structure; determined by how an object in LISP arranges the parts that comprise it. In AI, data structures in a program can change dynamically during program execution.

data tablet: a flat-surfaced graphic input unit used with a stylus for inking and cursor movement.

data-terminal equipment (DTE): that part of a station providing for the data-communication control function according to protocols.

data word: a unit of data stored in a single word of a storage medium.

DB: see *data base.*

DBMS: see *data base management system.*

DC: see *data channel.*

DCH: see *data channel.*

DDAS: see *digital data acquisition system.*

DDC: see *direct digital control.*

dead band: synonymous with *dead zone.*

dead zone: the range of input values for a signal that can be altered but has no impact on the output signal. synonymous with *dead band.*

debug: to detect, trace, and eliminate mistakes in computer programs or in other software. synonymous with *checkout.*

DEC: see *decimal.*

decimal (DEC)

(1) pertaining to a selection, choice, or condition that has 10 possible different values or states.

(2) pertaining to a fixed-radix numeration system having a radix of 10.

decimal digit: in decimal notation, or the decimal numeration system, one of the digits 0 to 9.

decimal notation: a notation that uses 10 different characters, usually the decimal digits; for example, the character string 196912312359 construed to represent the date and time one minute before the start of the year 1970. The representation used in the Universal Decimal Classification (UDC). cf. *decimal numeration system.*

decimal numeration system: the fixed-radix numeration system that uses the decimal digits and the radix 10 and in which the lowest integral weight is 1. cf. *decimal notation.*

decimal point: the radix point in the decimal numeration system. The decimal point may be represented, according to various conventions, by a comma, a period, or a point at the midheight of the digits.

decision instruction: synonymous with *branch instruction.*

decision table (DETAB)

(1) a presentation in either matrix or tabular form of a set of conditions and their corresponding actions.

(2) a table of all contingencies that are to be considered in the description of a problem, together with the actions to be taken for each set of contingencies.

decision tree: a discrimination network with a tree structure. see *discrimination network.*

deck: a collection of punched cards. A complete set of cards that have been punched for a particular purpose.

declaration section: the section of a computer program in which constructs such as data types, variables, procedures, and functions are announced and sometimes defined.

declarative knowledge: knowledge retrieved and stored that cannot be immediately executed; must be interpreted by procedural knowledge.

decode

(1) to convert data by reversing the effect of some previous encoding.

(2) in machine operation, to translate data and/or instructions to determine exactly how and where signals are to be sent.

(3) to interpret a code. cf. *encode.*

decoder (DEC)

(1) a device that decodes data.

(2) a device that has a number of input lines of which any number may carry signals, and a number of output lines of which not more than one may carry a signal, there being a one-to-one correspondence between the output and the combinations of the input signals. cf. *encoder.*

deductive inference: in formal logic, the derivation of a logical consequence from a specific set of premises; a truth-preserving transformation of assertions. see also *deductive inference rule.*

deductive inference rule: an inference rule that, provided with one or more assertions, determines a logically equivalent or more specific assertion. see *inference rule.*

deep knowledge: knowledge of basic theories, first principles, axioms, and facts about a domain. cf. *experiential knowledge.*

default value: the choice among exclusive alternatives made by the system when no explicit choice is specified by the user.

deferred addressing: a method of addressing in which one indirect address is replaced by another to which it refers a predetermined number of times, or until the process is terminated by an indicator.

degree of freedom: one of a limited number of ways in which a point or a body moves or in which a dynamic system changes, each way being expressed by an independent variable, and all required to be specified if the physical state of the body or system is to be completely defined.

delay: the amount of time by which an event is retarded.

demons: rules that fire automatically whenever a particular procedure is called.

DENDRAL: an early rule-based expert system that assists in determining organic-compound structure utilizing data from mass spectrometers and nuclear magnetic resonance devices. see also *META-DENDRAL.*

dependency: the relationship between a consequent and its antecedents that may require storage if the reasoning process is to be examined

47

retrospectively. A graph in which the nodes represent assertions and the arcs or other nodes represent relationships is called a *dependency network.*

dependency-directed backtracking: a programming method permitting a system to remove the effects of incorrect assumptions during its search for a solution to a problem. As the system infers new information, it keeps dependency records of all its deductions and assumptions, indicating how they were derived. When the system finds that an assumption was incorrect, it backtracks through the chains of inferences, removing conclusions based on the faulty assumption.

dependency network: see *dependency.*

depth-first search: in the hierarchy of rules or objects, a strategy in which one rule or object on the highest level is examined before the rules or objects immediately below it. Proceeding in this manner, the system searches down a single branch of the hierarchy tree until it ends. cf. *breadth-first search.*

derivative control: a control method whereby an actuator drive signal is proportional to the time derivative of the difference between the input (desired output) and the measured actual output.

description: synonymous with *concept description.*

descriptor: a variable, function, or predicate used as an elementary concept for describing objects or situations.

destructive read: reading that erases the data in the source location.

DETAB: see *decision table.*

detail card (deck): a card containing changeable information, as opposed to a master card or deck. Information from a master card is often transferred into a detail card at machine speed rather than by rekeying.

detail file: synonymous with *transaction file.*

detail printing

(1) printing information from each punched card passing through the unit.

(2) a means of printing where the accounting device prints one line per card.

development environment: a computer system designed to aid an individual in writing applications software. cf. *programming environment.*

diagnostic check: a specific routine designed to locate a malfunction in a computer.

diagnostic/prescriptive consultant paradigm: a pattern applied to problems requiring the user to identify symptoms or characteristics of a situation in order to determine which of several alternative solutions might be appropriate. Most expert systems and tools are designed to handle this paradigm.

diagnostic program: a computer program that recognizes, locates, and explains either a fault in equipment or a mistake in a computer program.

DIAL: Draper Industrial Assembly Language. A robot language developed at the Charles Stark Draper Laboratory at MIT for assembly tasks, utilizing a force sensor.

dichotomizing search: a search in which an ordered set of items is partitioned into two parts, one of which is rejected, the process being repeated on the accepted part until the search is completed. see also *binary search.*

differentiator: a device whose output function is proportional to the derivative of the input function with respect to one or more variables; for example, a resistance-capacitance network used to select the leading and trailing edges of a pulse signal.

DIG: see *digit.*

digit (DIG)

(1) a graphic character that represents an integer; for example, one of the characters 0 to 9.

(2) a symbol that represents one of the nonnegative integers smaller than the radix; for example, in decimal notation, a digit is one of the characters 0 to 9.

(3) synonymous with *numeric character.*

digital: denoting a discrete state of being such as the presence or absence of a quantity.

digital communications: the transfer of information via a sequence of signals, called bits, each of which has one of two different values. The signals may, for example, take the form of two different voltage levels on a wire or the presence or absence of light in a fiber-optic light guide. It can be made arbitrarily insensitive to external disturbances by means of error control methods.

digital computer

(1) a computer that operates on discrete data by performing arithmetic and logic processes on these data.

(2) a computer that consists of one or more associated processing

units and peripheral equipment, and that is controlled by internally stored programs. cf. *analog computer.*

digital control: an automated system using a digital computer or other digital elements for performing processing and control tasks for production systems.

digital data: data represented by digits, perhaps with special characters and the space characters.

digital data acquisition system (DDAS): a system found in plant floor automation for collecting digitized data, sometimes from limit switches, but usually from information inserted in work stations by means of punched cards and readable tags, as well as information inserted by the operator, using dials or a keyboard. The gathered data are used on dynamic inventory control for workflow monitoring and control, work measurement, and pay determination.

digital punch: any of the punches made in the 0 or 1 through 9 rows of the Hollerith card. The 1 through 9 digit punches are combined with the zone punches to make alphabet characters.

digital-to-analog converter (D/A) (DAC)
(1) a functional unit that converts digital data to analog signals.
(2) a device that converts a digital value to a proportional analog signal.

digitization: the process of converting an analog signal into digital values.

digitize: the analog-to-digital conversion of input from a video camera to a computer.

DIP: see *dual in-line package.*

dipmeter: see *dipmeter advisor.*

dipmeter advisor: an expert system that assists in analyzing dipmeter data. The dipmeter is used in the oil industry to determine subsurface tilt. The dipmeter produces tilt and tilt direction data as it moves through an oil well bore hole.

direct access: the facility to obtain data from a storage device, or to enter data into a storage device in such a way that the process depends only on the location of that data and not on a reference to data previously accessed.

direct-access storage: synonymous with *random-access storage.*

direct current (DC) motor: a motor that runs from a battery.

direct digital control (DDC): a computer control technique where a time-shared digital computer is substituted for a portion of or all of the analog simulator, thereby lowering capital investment and permitting greater facility in transferring a program from one system to another.

direct digital controller: a special purpose unit that replaces an analog set-point controller such as a flow-rate or temperature controller; compares a measured value to a set value and computes a correction signal.

direct drive: a unit where the joint shaft is directly coupled to the rotor of the drive motor without any gearing or other transmission mechanism.

directed activation: in an activation network, a technique for propagating the activation of one object by another. The activation network is a directed graph, indicating that propagation is to proceed only in accordance with the directed arcs.

direct insert subroutine: synonymous with *open subroutine.*

direct memory access (DMA): high-speed data transfer directly between an input/output channel and memory. synonymous with *cycle stealing; data break.*

direct numerical control (DNC)
(1) a situation in which a number of numerical control units are connected via a data transmission network. They can be under the direct control of a central computer, with or without the aid of an operator.
(2) using a computer for distribution of part program data (via data lines) to a plurality of remote, numerically controlled machine tools.

direct-view storage tube (DVST): a type of CRT with extremely long phosphor persistence.

discrete programming: synonymous with *integer programming.*

discrimination
(1) knowing which distinguishes instances of a concept from noninstances.
(2) the process of refining an overgeneralization of a concept to be learned so as to exclude noninstances that were once mistakenly classified as instances of the concept.
(3) a learning mechanism that exploits feedback concerning erroneous classifications for refining an overgeneralization of a concept.

discrimination instruction: an instruction of the class of instructions that comprises branch instructions and conditional jump instructions.

discrimination network: a network that encodes a set of tests for classifying a collection of objects into fixed categories, according to prede-termined features of the objects.

disjunction: the boolean operation whose result has the boolean value 0 if and only if each operand has the boolean value 0. synonymous with *inclusive-OR operation; logical ADD; OR operation.*

disk: loosely, a magnetic disk unit.

disk memories: millions of bits stored on horizontally stacked disks. Each disk contains a number of tracks, in each of which thousands of bits are recorded. A comb of vertical arms moves in and out of every disk simultaneously, stopping at the desired track, and reading or writing information from whatever disk is specified.

disk operating system: see *DOS.*

disk pack

(1)   a removable assembly of magnetic disks.

(2)   a portable set of flat, circular recording surfaces used in a disk storage device.

display console: a console that must include at least one display device and may also include one or more input units such as an alphanumeric keyboard, function keys, a job stick, a control ball, or a light pen.

display device

(1)   an output unit that gives a visual representation of data.

(2)   in computer graphics, a device capable of presenting display elements on a display surface; for example, a cathode-ray tube, plotter, microfilm viewer, or printer.

display station: a device for indicating alphanumeric information in a communications or computer system.

distal: away from the base, toward the end effector of the arm.

distributed control: a method whereby portions of a single control process are located in two or more places.

distributed function

(1)   the use of programmable terminals, controllers, and other devices to perform operations that were previously done by the processing unit such as managing data links, controlling devices, and formatting data.

(2)   functions such as network management, processing, and error recovery operations that are dispersed among the nodes of a network, as opposed to functions that are concentrated at a central location.

distributed processing: a technique for implementing a set of information processing functions within multiple physically separated physical devices.

disturbed circuit: see *crosstalk.*

disturbing circuitry: see *crosstalk.*

DL: see *data link.*

DMA: see *direct memory access.*

DMP: see *dump.*

DNC: see *direct numerical control.*

documentation: information that describes a computer program.

domain: a topical area or region of knowledge. Medicine, management science, and engineering are very broad domains. Existing knowledge systems only provide competent advice within very narrowly defined domains. synonymous with *task domain.*

domain expert: an individual who, through years of experience and training, has become extremely skilled at problem solving in a specific domain.

domain knowledge: knowledge about the problem domain (e.g., knowledge about geology in an expert system for discovering oil reserves).

domain of a descriptor: the set of possible values that a descriptor takes as part of a concept description. synonymous with *value set of a descriptor.*

do-nothing operation: synonymous with *no-operation instruction.*

DOS: Disk Operating System. A program that controls the computer's transfer of data to and from a hard or floppy disk. Frequently combined with the main operating system.

DOS/VS: Disk Operating System with Virtual Storage.

dot printer: synonymous with *matrix printer.*

double precision: the use of two computer words to represent a number in accordance with the required precision.

double-rail logic: pertaining to self-timing asynchronous circuits in which each logic variable is represented by two electrical lines which together can take on three meaningful states: zero, one, and undecided.

double-word (DW): a contiguous sequence of bits or characters that comprises two computer words and is capable of being addressed as a unit.

download: transferring information electronically from a larger or more sophisticated system to a simpler one.

Draper Industrial Assembly Language: see *DIAL.*

drift
(1)   a change in the output of a circuit that occurs slowly.
(2)   the tendency of a system's response to move gradually away from the desired response.
drive motors: main motors in a robot that control body movement.
drop-in
(1)   the reading of a spurious signal whose amplitude is greater than a predetermined percentage of the nominal signal.
(2)   an error in the storage into or the retrieval from a magnetic storage device, revealed by the reading of a binary character not previously recorded. Drop-ins are usually caused by defects in, or the presence of particles on, the magnetic surface layer.
drop-out
(1)   in magnetic tape, a recorded signal whose amplitude is less than a predetermined percentage of a reference signal.
(2)   in data communication, a momentary loss in signal, usually due to noise or system malfunction.
(3)   a failure to read a bit from magnetic storage.
(4)   an error in the storage into or the retrieval from a magnetic storage device, revealed by a failure to read a binary character. Drop-outs are usually caused by defects in, or the presence of particles on, the magnetic surface layer.
drum memory: a storage unit used for auxiliary memory. The device resembles a drum and information is stored magnetically on its surface.
drum sequencer: a mechanical programming unit used to operate limit switches or valves to control a robot.
DTE: see *data-terminal equipment.*
dual in-line package (DIP):   a standard integrated circuit enclosed in a molded plastic unit. Consists of two parallel rows of pins connected to the circuit board. Such circuits are the foundation of integrated circuit boards.
dual semantics: a concept in which a computer program can be viewed from either of two equally valid perspectives: procedural semantics (what happens when the program is run) and declarative semantics (what knowledge the program contains).
dump (DMP)
(1)   data that have been dumped.
(2)   to write the contents of a storage, or of part of a storage (usually

54

from an internal storage to an external medium) for a specific purpose such as to allow other use of the storage as a safeguard against faults or errors, or in connection with debugging.

duodecimal

(1)   characterized by a selection, choice, or condition that has 12 possible values or states.

(2)   pertaining to a fixed-radix numeration system having a radix of 12.

duplex: in data communication, a simultaneous two-way independent transmission in both directions. synonymous with *full duplex*. cf. *half-duplex*.

duty cycle: the fraction of time during which a unit or system is active or at full power.

DVST: see *direct-view storage tube*.

DW: see *double-word*.

dyadic boolean operation: a boolean operation on two operands. synonymous with *binary boolean operation*.

dyadic operation: synonymous with *binary arithmetic operation*.

dyadic operator: an operator that represents an operation on two operands. The dyadic operators are AND, equivalence, exclusion, exclusive OR, inclusion, NAND, NOR, and OR. synonymous with *binary operator*.

dynabook: an early specification for a book-sized computer for education and entertainment.

dynamic accuracy

(1)   accuracy determined with a time-varying output.

(2)   the difference between actual position response and position desired or commanded of an automatic control system as measured during motion.

dynamic behavior: how a system performs with respect to time.

dynamic dump: dumping performed during the execution of a computer program, usually under the control of that computer program.

dynamic-free variables: in LISP, in the context of calling a function, a value that is not necessarily restricted to one environment; that is, the variable can be bound within several environments. cf. *lexical-free variables*.

dynamic knowledge base: see *short-term memory*.

dynamic linking: in LISP, values linked with variables when a function is called, not when a function is defined.

55

dynamic memory: synonymous with *dynamic storage.*

dynamic memory allocation: in LISP, where memory management is fully automatic and occurs during run times, and where values are assigned to variables when a program is executed, not before.

dynamic programming: in operations research, a procedure for optimization of a multistage problem solution wherein a number of decisions are available to each stage of the process. cf. *convex programming; linear programming.*

dynamic range: a range of signals, from weakest to strongest, which a receiver is able to accept as input.

dynamic storage

(1)   a device storing data in a manner that permits the data to move or vary with time so that the specified data are not always available for recovery. Magnetic drum storage and disk storage are dynamic non-volatile storage. An acoustic delay line is a dynamic volatile storage.

(2)   the available storage left within the partition after the task set is loaded. synonymous with *dynamic memory.*

E

EA: see *effective address.*

EBCDIC: Extended Binary-Coded Decimal Interchange Code. A coded character set consisting of 8-bit coded characters which provides capacity for both upper- and lowercase letters, numerals and other special characters, as well as unused configurations for future use.

echo check: a procedure to determine the correctness of a transmission of data in which the received data are returned to the source for comparison with the originally transmitted data.

EDD: expert data base designer. A Prolog-based expert system.

edge: the distinguishable change in pixel values between two regions. Edges correspond to changes in brightness from a discontinuity in surface reflection or illumination.

edit

(1) to prepare data for a later operation. Editing may include the rearrangement or the addition of data, the deletion of unwanted data, format control, code conversion, and the application of standard processes such as zero suppression.

(2) to enter, modify, or delete data.

editor program: a computer program designed to perform such functions as the rearrangement, modification, and deletion of data in accordance with prescribed rules.

EDP: see *electronic data processing.*

effective address (EA)

(1) the contents of the address part of an effective instruction.

(2) the address that is derived by applying any specified indexing or indirect addressing rules to the specified address, and that is actually used to identify the current operand.

effector: apparatus used to produce a desired response (from a shift in its input) on another unit where the end result is needed.

Electrically Programmable Read Only Memory: see *EPROM.*

electronic data processing (EDP): data processing largely performed by electronic devices.

electrooptical imaging sensors: sensors used as "eyes" for industrial robots and visual inspection. Standard television cameras, using vidicons, plumbicons, and silicon target vidicons, interface with a computer and provide the least expensive and most easily available imaging sensors.

ELEM: see *element.*

element (ELEM) (ELT)

(1) in a set, an object, entity, or concept having the properties that define a set. synonymous with *member.*

(2) the particular resource within a subarea that is identified by an element address.

element class: the data type of a working memory element.

element variable: a variable bound to an entire working memory element, instead of to the values of that element's attributes.

elevation: the direction of a straight line to a point in a vertical plane, expressed as the angular distance from a reference line such as the observer's line of view.

ELT: see *element.*

EM: see *end-medium character.*

emulation

(1) the imitation of all or part of one computer system by another (primarily by hardware), so that the imitating computer system accepts the same data, executes the same programs, and achieves the same results as the imitated computer system.

(2) the use of programming techniques and special machine features to permit a computing system to execute programs written for another system.

EMYCIN: the first expert system building tool; derived from the expert system MYCIN. After the developers of MYCIN completed that system, they attempted to remove the specific medical knowledge from MYCIN (hence, Essential MYCIN). The resulting shell consisted of a back-chaining inference engine, a consultation driver, and several knowledge acquisition aids. This shell, or tool, is then combined with another knowledge base, creating a new expert system. see also *context tree; context-parameter-value triplets; MYCIN.*

encode: to convert data by the use of a code or a coded character set in such a manner that reconversion to the original form is possible. This term is sometimes loosely used when complete reconversion is not possible. cf. *decode.*

encoder

(1)　a device that encodes data.

(2)　a device that has a number of input lines of which not more than one at a time may carry a signal, and a number of output lines of which any number may carry signals, there being a one-to-one correspondence between the combinations of output signals and input signals. cf. *decoder.*

end-around borrow:　the action of transferring a borrow digit from the most significant digit place to the least significant digit place.

end-around carry:　the action of transferring a carry digit from the most significant digit place to the least significant digit place. An end-around carry may be necessary when adding two negative numbers that are represented by their diminished radix complements.

end effector:　an actuator, gripper, or driven mechanical unit attached to the end of a manipulator by which objects can be grasped or otherwise acted upon. see also *gripper.*

end-medium character (EM):　a control character used to identify the physical end of the data medium, the end of the used portion of the medium, or the end of the wanted portion of the data recorded on the medium.

end of address (EOA):　one or more control characters transmitted on a line to indicate the end of nontext characters; for example, addressing characters.

end of arm speed:　the arm speed depending on the axes about which the arm is moving, its position in the work envelope, and the load being carried.

end-point control:　synonymous with *coordinated axis control.*

end-point rigidity:　the resistance of the hand, tool, or end point of a manipulator arm to motion under applied force.

end-user:　an individual using the finished expert system; the individual for whom the system was developed.

ENQ:　see *enquiry character.*

enquiry character (ENQ):　a transmission control character used as a request for a response from the station with which the connection has

59

been set up; the response may include station identification, the type of equipment in service, and the status of the remote station.

entrance: synonymous with *entry point.*

entry: synonymous with *entry point.*

entry point

(1) the address of the label of the first instruction executed on entering a computer program, a routine, or a subroutine. A computer program, a routine, or a subroutine may have a number of different entry points, each perhaps corresponding to a different function or purpose. synonymous with *entrance; entry.*

(2) in a routine, any place to which control can be passed.

envelope

(1) a group of binary digits formed by a byte and augmented by a number of additional bits which are required for the operation of the data network.

(2) the total space that a robot arm can reach: up, out, down, and side to side. see also *working envelope.*

environment: see *programming environment.*

Envisage: the second generation of a Prolog-derived tool, originally called SAGE. Contains the feel of Prolog, but also has rules that fire automatically whenever a particular procedure is called; this feature allows the user to suspend one line of questioning temporarily and reanswer another set of questions to compare results.

EPROM (erasable PROM): Electrically Programmable Read Only Memory. Has permanent data electrically recorded or programmed into it, and therefore can only be read.

equivalence: a logic operator having the property that if *P* is a statement, *Q* is a statement, and *R* is a statement, then the equivalence of *P, Q, R, . . .* is true if and only if all statements are true, or all statements are false.

equivalence operation: the dyadic boolean operation whose result has the boolean value 1 if and only if the operands have the same boolean value. synonymous with *IF-AND-ONLY-IF operation.*

equivalent-binary-digit-factor: the average number of binary digits required to express one radix digit in a nonbinary numeration system. For example, approximately three and one-third times the number of decimal digits is required to express a decimal numeral as a binary numeral.

erasable PROM: see *EPROM.*

erase

(1)   to remove data from a data medium, leaving the medium available for recording new data.

(2)   to remove all previous data from magnetic storage by changing it to a specified condition; this may be an unmagnetized state or a pre-determined magnetized state.

error burst: in data communication, a sequence of signals containing one or more errors, but counted as only one unit in accordance with some specific criterion or measure. An example of such a criterion could be that if three consecutive correct bits follow an erroneous bit, then an error burst is terminated.

error control procedure: the inclusion of redundant information in a message (e.g., parity bits, check sums, cyclic redundancy check characters, and fire) to permit the detection of errors that arise from noise or other disturbances in the transmission medium.

error correcting code

(1)   an error-detecting code designed to correct certain kinds of errors.

(2)   a code in which each telegraph or data signal conforms to specific rules of construction so that departures from this construction in the receive signals can be automatically detected, permitting the automatic correction, at the receiving terminal, of some or all of the errors. Such codes require more signal elements than are necessary to convey the basic information.

error signal: a signal whose magnitude and sign are used to correct the alignment between the controlling and the controlled elements of an automatic control unit.

ES: see *expert system.*

ESC: see *escape character.*

escape character (ESC):   a code extension character used, in some cases, with one or more succeeding characters to indicate (by some convention or agreement) that the coded representations following the character or the group of characters are to be interpreted according to a different code or according to a different coded character set.

ESE/VM: see *Expert System Environment/VM.*

Essential MYCIN: see *EMYCIN.*

Ethernet: a local network that sends messages between computers by way of a single coaxial cable which snakes through all of the computers

61

to be connected. A coaxial cable is a cable consisting of a central wire surrounded by a grounded cylindrical shielding sheath.

EVAL function: see *read-eval-print loop.*

evaluation function: a method for determining the value or worth of proposed intermediate steps during a hunt through a search space for a solution to a problem.

EX: see *execute.*

example-driven system: synonymous with *induction system.*

exception: an abnormal condition such as an I/O error encountered in processing a data set or a file.

excess-three code: the binary-coded decimal notation in which a decimal digit n is represented by the binary numeral that represents $(n + 3)$.

exclusion

(1) the dyadic boolean operation whose result has the boolean value if and only if the first operand has the boolean value 1 and the second has the boolean value 0.

(2) a logic operator having the property that if P is a statement and Q is a statement, then P exclusion Q is true if P is true and Q is false, false if P is false, and false if both statements are true. P exclusion Q is often represented by a combination of "AND" and "NOT" symbols such as $P \ Q$. synonymous with *NOT-IF-THEN operation.*

EXEC: see *execute.*

execute (EX) (EXEC)

(1) to perform the execution of an instruction or of a computer program.

(2) in programming, to change the state of a computer in accordance with the rules of the operations it recognizes.

execute phase: the logical subdivision of a run that includes the execution of the target program. synonymous with *executing phase.*

executing phase: synonymous with *execute phase.*

execution: the running of a program or the carrying out of the operator instructions.

execution-driven reasoning: a method using current data and decision for building hypotheses about pending, unobserved events; allocates resources to activities that confirm and monitor the expected events.

execution stack: in a language, a segment of memory containing values of variables. The values are pulled from the stack or pushed onto the stack, according to how the language is implemented during execution of a program or a call to a function.

executive program: synonymous with *supervisory program.*

exhaustive search: a procedure in which each path through a decision tree or network is examined.

exit: an instruction in a computer program, a routine, or a subroutine. Once this instruction is executed, control is no longer exercised by that computer program, routine, or subroutine.

exoskeleton: an articular mechanism whose joints correspond to those of a human arm, and when attached to the arm of a human operator, will move in correspondence to his or her arm. Exoskeletal devices are sometimes instrumented and used for master/slave control of manipulators.

expansion card: a card that enables other electronic units to be added to the system.

expectation-driven reasoning: a problem-solving method that generates hypotheses about events that are expected to occur, and focuses processing on tasks related to these events.

experiential knowledge: knowledge gained from hands-on experience, consisting of specific facts and rules of thumb. cf. *deep knowledge.* synonymous with *heuristic knowledge; surface knowledge.*

expert data base designer: see *EDD.*

expertise: skill and knowledge possessed by humans resulting in performance far above the norm; consists of massive amounts of information combined with rules of thumb, simplifications, rare facts, and wise procedures in such a fashion that a person can analyze specific types of problems in an efficient way.

expertise acquisition: synonymous with *knowledge acquisition.*

expert system (ES)

(1) a computer system that can perform at, or near, the level of a human expert.

(2) any computer system developed by means of a loose collection of techniques associated with artificial intelligence research. Therefore, any computer system developed by means of an expert system building tool (even were the system to be so narrowly constrained that it could never be said to rival a human expert). see also *knowledge system.*

(3) a computer program that performs a specialized, usually difficult professional task at the level of (or sometimes beyond the level of) a

human expert. Because their functioning relies heavily on large bodies of knowledge, expert systems are sometimes known as *knowledge-based systems.* Since they are often used to assist the human expert, they are also known as *intelligent assistants.* see also *knowledge base management system; symbolic inference.*

expert system-building tool: the programming language and support package for building an expert system.

Expert System Environment/VM (ESE/VM): IBM's first entry into the expert systems tools market, with two subtools: one is essentially the knowledge engineering interface, and the other, the inference engine and the user interface. Also provides a good set of utilities that allow the knowledge engineer to control the user interface and use graphics when desired.

explanation: information presented to justify a specific course of reasoning or action. In knowledge systems, a number of techniques that help a user understand what a system is doing. Many knowledge systems permit a user to ask "Why," "How," or "Explain." In each case, the system responds by revealing something about its assumptions or its inner reasoning.

explanation facility: the portion of an expert system that explains how solutions were arrived at and justifies the steps used in reaching them.

explicit address: synonymous with *absolute address.*

exponent: in a floating-point representation, the numeral that denotes the power to which the implicit floating-point base is raised before being multiplied by the fixed-point part to determine the real number represented; for example, a floating-point representation of the number 0.0001234 is 0.1234-3, where 0.1234 is the fixed-point part and -3 is the exponent.

EXPRESS: a sophisticated financial modeling system.

Extended Binary-Coded Decimal Interchange Code: see *EBCDIC.*

extensible: in a computer language or in some software, the existing features of the language or software used for adding new, and integrated, features. LISP is an extensible computer language.

extension: the orientation or motion toward a position where the joint angle between two connected bodies is 180°.

external devices: another computer, with full capability for supplemental program management, enhancing the computer-controlled robot's capacity for making decisions, or its capacity for programmed points.

The external computer need not be dedicated to just communicating with one robot. It could be a computer that already exists within the application, in which case its duties are expanded to include communicating with the robot.

external sensor: a sensor for measuring displacements, forces, or other variables in the environment external to a robot.

external sort

(1) a sort that requires the use of auxiliary storage because the set of items to be sorted cannot all be held in the available internal storage at one time.

(2) a sort program, or a sort phase of a multipass sort, that merges strings of items, using auxiliary storage, until one string is formed.

external storage

(1) storage that is accessible by a computer only through input/output channels.

(2) in a hierarchy of storage devices of a data processing system, any storage device that is not internal storage. External storage and internal storage are terms which take on precise meanings only with reference to a particular configuration.

Ex-Tran 7: a combination inductive and rule-based tool to which rules can either be inferred from examples or entered directly.

F: see *file*.

FA: see *full adder*.

face-change character: synonymous with *font-change character*.

fact: a statement whose validity is accepted. In most knowledge systems a fact consists of an attribute and a specific associated value.

factory: an Integrated Computer-Aided Manufacturing unit consisting of a number of centers and the materials transport, storage buffers, and communications that interconnect them.

factory control: a module in the Integrated Computer-Aided Manufacturing hierarchy for controlling a factory, which is controlled by management personnel and policies.

fail-safe: term used to describe a system which is able to close down in a controlled fashion during a serious failure, although some deterioration in performance can be expected. synonymous with *fail soft*.

fail soft: synonymous with *fail-safe*.

false add: to form a partial sum; that is, to add without carries.

Fast Reading and Understanding Memory Program: see *FRUMP*.

FC: see *font change character*.

FCT: see *function*.

feature: see *attribute*.

feedback: the return of part of the output of a machine, process, or system to the computer as input for another phase, especially for self-correcting or control purposes.

feedback control: a guidance technique used by robots to bring the end effector to a programmed point.

feedback devices: digital or analog units for sensing the positions of the various links and joints of a robot, and for transmitting this information to the controller.

feedback loop: the components and processes involved in correcting and/or controlling a system by using part of the output as input.

feed-forward control: see *continuous-path control.*

FEFO: see *first-ended, first-out.*

fembot: a humanoid robot given female sex characteristics or a female orientation.

ferromagnetic: the capability of some materials to be highly magnetized and exhibit hysteresis (e.g., iron and nickel).

fetch

(1) to locate and load a quantity of data from storage.

(2) in virtual storage systems, to bring load modules or program phases from auxiliary storage into virtual storage.

(3) a control program routine that accomplishes (1) or (2).

(4) synonymous with *retrieve.*

FF: see *flip-flop.*

fiber optics: a communication method where information is transmitted in the form of light over a transparent fiber material such as a strand of glass. Advantages are noise-free communication not susceptible to electromagnetic interference.

Fibonacci series: a series of integers in which each integer is equal to the sum of the two preceding integers in the series.

fiduciary object: a feature of an environment that a robot system uses as a reference point for establishing its own position.

field (FLD)

(1) in a record, a specified area used for a particular category of data; for example, a group of card columns in which a wage rate is recorded.

(2) a group of adjacent card columns on a punch card.

(3) in a data base, the smallest unit of data that can be referred to.

field testing: the fifth phase in knowledge engineering; involves testing the system in user environments and modifying and polishing the system until it performs as desired. For other phases see *knowledge engineering.*

fifth generation: a name first used by the Japanese for an ambitious program to achieve supremacy in the computer business. This generation of equipment separated from earlier generations by higher speed and employment of artificial intelligence.

file (F): a set of related records treated as a unit; for example, in stock control, a file could consist of a set of invoices.

filtering: the exclusion of either data (data filtering) or rules (rule filtering) from the match process for the sake of efficiency.

fire: to execute the set of actions identified in the right-hand side of an instantiation of a rule.

firmware (FW): a computer's components that are neither hardware or software; for example, a unit for storing information used in programming the computer.

first-ended, first-out (FEFO): a queuing scheme whereby messages on a destination queue are sent to the destination on a first-ended, first-out basis within priority groups. That is, higher priority messages are sent before lower priority messages; when two messages on a queue have equal priority, the one whose final segment arrived at the queue earliest is sent first.

first-generation computer: a computer utilizing vacuum tube components.

first-level message: under a time-sharing option, a diagnostic message for identifying a general condition; more specific information is issued in a second-level message if the text is followed by a " + ."

five-bit byte: synonymous with *quintet*.

fixed coordinate system: a coordinate system fixed in time.

fixed-length commands: computer commands having the same length.

fixed-point part: synonymous with *mantissa*.

fixed-point representation: a radix numeration system in which the radix point is implicitly fixed in the series of digit places by some convention on which agreement has been reached.

fixed-radix numeration system: a radix numeration system in which all the digit places, except perhaps the one with the highest weight, have the same radix. The weights of successive digit places are successive integral powers of a single radix, each multiplied by the same factor. Negative integral powers of the radix are used in the representation of fractions. A fixed-radix numeration system is a particular case of a mixed-radix numeration system.

fixed-stop robot: a robot with a stop-point control but having no trajectory control. Although efficient repeatability is created, the robot is unable to stop at more than two locations.

fixed storage: synonymous with *read-only memory*.

fixed-word length computer: a computer in which data is treated in units of a fixed number of characters or bits.

fixture: a device for holding and locating a workpiece during inspection or production operations.

flag (FLG)
    (1)   any of various types of indicators used for identification; for example, a wordmark.
    (2)   a character that signals the occurrence of some condition such as the end of a word.
    (3)   synonym for *sentinel; switch indicator.*

flag bit: a bit which specifically indicates a condition or status to be met by arithmetic operations; for example, carry, overflow, zero, sign, parity.

flavor: in LISP software, objects and methods which, collectively, provide object-oriented programming.

FLD: see *field.*

flexibility: the ease with which a robot adjusts itself to changes in manufacturing tasks. cf. *hard automation.*

flexible manufacturing system (FMS):   a system which utilizes robot-controlled transport of work from one machine to another. Control is provided by numerical control units connected into a computer numerical control system.

flexion: an orientation or motion toward a position where the joint angle between two connected bodies is small.

FLG: see *flag.*

flicker: the dimming of a CRT display prior to each refresh, caused when refresh rate falls below the phosphor persistence.

flip-flop (FF):   a circuit or device containing active elements, capable of assuming either one of two stable states at a given time. synonymous with *toggle.*

floating point: a system of representing numerical quantities with a variable number of places in which the location of the point does not remain fixed.

floating-point base: in a floating-point representation system, the implicit fixed positive integer base, greater than unity, that is raised to the power explicitly denoted by the exponent in the floating-point representation or represented by the characteristic in the floating-point representation and then multiplied by the fixed-point part to determine the real number represented; for example, in the floating-point representation of the number 0.0001234, namely 0.1234-3, the implicit floating-point base is 10. synonymous with *floating-point radix.*

floating-point radix: synonymous with *floating-point base.*

floating-point representation: a representation of a real number in a

70

floating-point representation system; for example, a floating-point representation of the number 0.0001234 is 0.1234-3, where 0.1234 is the fixed-point part and -3 is the exponent. The numerals are expressed in the variable-point decimal numeration system. cf. *variable-point representation.*

floor-to-floor time: the total time elapsed in picking up a part, loading it into a machine, carrying out operations, and unloading it (back to the floor, bin pallet, etc.); usually applies to batch production.

fluerics: the area within the field of fluidics in which components and systems perform functions such as sensing, logic, amplification, and control without the use of mechanical parts.

fluidic: pertaining to the sensing, control information processing, and actuation functions performed through the use of fluid dynamic phenomena.

FMS: see *flexible manufacturing system.*

FOCUS: a sophisticated language for data base interaction.

font: a set of type of a specific size and face. The face is the style and proportion of a symbol. Size is stated in points: 8 point, 10 point, 12 point, and so on.

font-change character (FC):   a control character that selects and makes effective a change in the specific shape and/or size of graphics, the character set remaining unchanged. synonymous with *face-change character.*

font editor: in software, a function that allows an individual to alter the font used to display text or print files.

force and torque sensors: sensors that directly measure the force and torque acting on each point of a manipulator. If the joint is driven by an electric DC motor, sensing is done by measuring the armature current. If driven by a hydraulic motor, then sensing is done by measuring the back pressure. Accuracy and resolution of this measurement are adversely affected by the variability in the inertia of the arm and its load, and by the nonuniform friction of the individual joints.

force feedback: a sensing method using electrical or hydraulic signals for controlling a robot end effector.

force sensor: a sensor able to measure the forces and torques exerted by a robot at its wrist. When mounted in the work surface, rather than the robot's wrist, such a sensor is called a pedestal sensor.

forearm: the link which is connected to the wrist.

foreground processing: the execution of a computer program that pre-empts the use of computer facilities. cf. *background processing.*

format: the arrangement or layout of data on a data medium.

form feed: paper throw used to bring an assigned part of a form to the printing position.

formula translation: see *FORTRAN.*

FORTH: a computer language that is fast and which is used to control devices in real time.

FORTRAN (formula translation)

(1)   a programming language primarily used to express computer programs by arithmetic formulas.

(2)   a programming language primarily designed for applications involving numeric computations.

FORTRAN IV: a refinement of the original FORTRAN, employing a wider range of symbols and instruction statements. Allows for more accuracy and flexibility because program statements and numbers can be longer. It requires a compiler.

forward chaining: a control strategy that regulates the order in which inferences are drawn. In a rule-based system, it begins by asserting all of the rules whose *if* clauses are true. It then checks to determine what additional rules might be true, given the facts it has already established. The process is repeated until the program reaches a goal or runs out of new possibilities. synonymous with *data driven.*

four-address: pertaining to an instruction format containing four address parts.

four-bit byte: synonymous with *quartet.*

four-plus-one address: pertaining to an instruction that contains four operand addresses and the address of the next instruction to be executed.

frame: a knowledge representation scheme that associates an object with a collection of features (e.g., facts, rules, etc.). Each feature is stored in a slot. A frame is the set of slots related to a specific object; it is similar to a property list, schema, or record (which are used in conventional programming). synonymous with *object; unit.*

frame-based methods: programming techniques utilizing frame hierarchies for inheritance and procedural attachment.

frame buffer: a memory device which stores the contents of an image pixel by pixel. Frame buffers are used to refresh a raster image. The "depth" of the frame buffer is the number of bits per pixel, which determines the number of colors or intensities which can be displayed.

Franz LISP: a dialect of LISP.

FRED: Front End for Databases. A system which is a knowledge-based cooperative man–machine communication assistant.

free variable: in LISP, in the context of calling a function, a free variable is an atom not found in a function's parameter list.

frequency response

(1) the capability of a specific circuit or unit to carry signals of different frequencies.

(2) the response of a dynamic system to a sinusoid.

(3) the characterization of response of a dynamic system to any periodic signal according to the Fourier coefficient or the gain-and-phase at each frequency multiple of the period.

front end analysis: the first phase in knowledge engineering; involves all of the questions to be asked before beginning an expert system project, to determine if an expert system is appropriate to a task, would be cost effective, and so on. Also to be identified are sponsors and arrange-to-manage expectations. In addition, the groundwork needed for the success of any costly software development project must be done. For other phases see *knowledge engineering.*

Front End for Databases: see *FRED.*

FRUMP: Fast Reading and Understanding Memory Program. An experimental language-understanding system for scanning the UPI newswire, and locating and summarizing stories belonging to certain classes.

full adder (FA): a combination circuit that has three inputs which are augend (D), addend (E), and a carry digit transferred from another digit place (F). Its two outputs are a sum without carry (T), and a new carry digit (R). In this circuit, the outputs are related to the inputs. synonymous with *three-input adder.*

full duplex: synonymous with *duplex.*

full subtractor: a combinational circuit that has three inputs: a minuend (I), a subtrahend (J), and a borrow digit (K) transferred from another digit place. Its two outputs are a difference (W), and a new borrow digit (X). In this circuit the outputs are related to the inputs.

full word: synonymous with *word.*

FUNC: see *function.*

function (FCT) (FUNC)

(1)   a mathematical entity whose value (i.e., the value of the dependent variable) depends in a specified manner on the values of one or more independent variables, with not more than one or more independent variables corresponding to each permissible combination of values from the respective ranges of the independent variables.

(2)   a specific purpose of an entity, or its characteristic action.

(3)   a subroutine that returns the value of a single variable, and that usually has a single exit; for example, subroutines that compute mathematical functions such as sine, cosine, and logarithm, or that compute the maximum of a set of numbers.

function call: in LISP, returning a value that can be used by the program; for example, a program that searches through a data base for finding people in a certain category might call a function that alphabetized the individual's names before the program prints their names. synonymous with *calling a function*.

function table

(1)   two or more sets of data so arranged that an entry in one set selects one or more entries in the remaining sets; for example, a tabulation of the values of a function for a set of values of the variable; that is, a dictionary.

(2)   a hardware device, or a subroutine that can either decode multiple inputs into a single output, or encode a single input into multiple outputs.

fuzzy logic: an approach to approximate reasoning in which truth values and quantifiers are defined as possibility distributions that carry linguistic labels such as true, very true, not very true, many, not very many, few, and several.

FW: see *firmware*.

G

G: see *giga-*.

gain: the amount of increase in a signal as it passes through a control system or a specific control element. If a signal gets smaller, it is said to be attenuated.

gang punch: to punch identical data into a card deck.

gantry robot: a robot suspended from a bridgelike framework.

gap character: a character that is included in a computer word for technical reasons, but which does not represent data.

garbage collecting (collection): in LISP, a method for removing unneeded bindings, refreshing pointers, and reallocating memory. Following garbage collection, reclaimed memory is available for binding variables.

garbage in, garbage out: see *GIGO*.

gas panel: synonymous with *plasma panel*.

gate
(1)   a combinational circuit with only one output channel.
(2)   a device having one output channel and one or more input channels, such that the output channel state is completely determined by the input channel states, except during switching transients.

gate-array technology: an approach to integrated circuit design. The circuit designer, rather than beginning over with a blank slate each time, adds specializing detail to a partially wired array of basic circuit elements.

G-byte: see *Gigabytes*.

gears: wheels with teeth used to transmit power from motor to wheel.

GEN: see *generation*.

generalization: synonymous with *concept description*.

generalization rule: an inference rule for transforming one or more premise assertions into an assertion that logically implies them.

general-purpose computer (GPC): a computer that is designed to operate on a wide variety of problems.

general-purpose knowledge engineering language: a computer language designed for building expert systems and incorporating features that make it applicable to different problem areas and types.

generate and test: a problem-solving method using a generator that produces possible solutions and an evaluator that tests the acceptability of those solutions.

generated address: an address that has been formed as a result of the execution of a computer program. synonymous with *synthetic address*.

generating function: in a series of functions or constants, a mathematical function that, when represented by an infinite series, has those functions or constants as coefficients in the series.

generation (GEN)

(1) a differentiation of the ages to which equipment belongs.

(2) in micrographics, a measure of the remoteness of the copy from the original material, the first microfilm representation being the first generation microfilm.

generation 1 robot: a robot characterized by a programmable, memory-controlled unit with several degrees of freedom that is usually equipped with grippers for holding and operating various tools. cf. *generation 1.5 robot; generation 2 robot; generation 3 robot*.

generation 1.5 robot: a robot that is sensory-controlled and able to carry out "make" and "test" activities. These robots are memory-controlled, with overrides of preprogrammed control based on sensor inputs. cf. *generation 1 robot; generation 2 robot; generation 3 robot*.

generation 2 robot: a future stage robot possessing hand-and-eye coordination control through machine-vision concepts able to perceive objects, and with hand interactions capable of performing manipulative tasks. cf. *generation 1 robot; generation 1.5 robot; generation 3 robot*.

generation 3 robot: a future, factory intelligence-controlled robot able to provide artificial intelligence for solving factory tasks. cf. *generation 1 robot; generation 1.5 robot; generation 2 robot*.

generative grammar: a formal grammar of a language expressed as a set of rules that is applied to generate all the sentences of the language and no sentences that are not in that language.

generator: a controlling routine that performs a generating function; for example, report generator, I/O generator.

giga- (G): ten to the ninth power, 1,000,000,000 in decimal notation. When referring to storage capacity, two to the thirtieth power, 1,073,741,824 in decimal notation.

Gigabytes (G-byte): the number of bytes given by 2 raised to the 30th power, or 1,073,741,824 bytes, or 1.073741824 billion bytes. The storage capacity of a large AI system reaches the G-byte level.

GIGO: garbage in, garbage out. The acronymic expression of the concept that results produced from unreliable or useless data are equally unreliable or useless.

GM: see *groupmark*.

goal: the end to which problem solving aspires. In a production system, it is represented in a separate memory or in a distinguished class of working memory elements. synonymous with *task*.

goal-directed: synonymous with *backward chaining*.

goal-directed inference: see *inference, goal-directed*.

goal tree: a tree data structure wherein the root node represent a goal to be achieved, and the children of each goal represent subgoals that, when achieved, suffice to achieve the goal represented by their parent. A goal tree can be an and/or tree. see also *and/or tree*.

Golem: a fictitious robot made from clay.

GOTO-less programming: synonymous with *structured programming*.

GPC: see *general-purpose computer*.

graceful degradation

(1) attaining an acceptable level of reduced service.

(2) the decline in performance of a component part of a system without immediate and significant decline in performance of the system as a whole and/or decline in the quality of the product.

graceful failure: the failure in performance of a component part of a system without immediate major interruption or failure of performance of the system as a whole, and/or sacrifice in quality of the product.

grammatical inference: inferring the grammar of a language, given a set of sentences that are grammatically correct, and a second (optional) set that are grammatically incorrect.

granularity: the level of detail in a chunk of information (e.g., a rule or frame).

graphic: a symbol produced by a process such as handwriting, drawing, or printing. synonymous with *graphic symbol*.

graphic symbol: synonymous with *graphic*.

gray code: a binary code in which sequential numbers are represented by binary expressions, each of which differs from the preceding expression in one place only. synonymous with *reflected binary code*.

gray level: a quantitized measurement of pixel brightness.

gray-scale images: the hierarchy of solid continuous blocks of single tones that may be combined in different sizes and forms to represent an image.

grid: in optical character recognition, two mutually orthogonal sets of parallel lines used for specifying or measuring character images.

gripper: an actuator or mechanical device attached to the wrist of a manipulator, by which objects can be grasped or otherwise acted on.

group classification codes: system classification with categories under each classification represented by the assignment of succeeding digits. Used for coding classes of products, accounts, and items in which division of groups under a major heading is the primary goal.

group identification: printed information identifying a group of data.

groupmark (group mark) (GM): a mark that identifies the beginning or the end of a set of data, which may include blocks, characters, or other items.

group printing

(1) a machine activity in which not every card is printed. Instead, it summarizes the data held in a group of cards and prints only the summarized totals.

(2) printing one line of information for a specific group.

group technology

(1) a system for coding parts based on similarities in geometrical shape or other characteristics.

(2) the grouping of parts into families based on similarities in their production, so that the parts of a particular family can then be processed together.

H

H: see *head*.

HA: see *half-adder*.

half-adder (HA): a combinational circuit that has two inputs, *A* and *B*, and two outputs, one being a sum without carry, *S*, and the other being a carry, *C*, and in which the outputs are related to the inputs.

half-adjust: to round by one-half of the maximum value of the number base of the counter. see also *round*.

half-duplex (HD) (HDX): in data communication, pertaining to an alternate, single direction, independent transmission. cf. *duplex*.

half-subtractor (HS): a combinational circuit that has two inputs which are minuend (*G*), subtrahend (*H*), and two outputs which are a difference (*U*), and a borrow digit (*V*). In this circuit, the outputs are related to the inputs.

halfword (half-word): a contiguous sequence of bits or characters which comprises half a computer word and is capable of being addressed as a unit.

halt instruction: synonymous with *pause instruction*.

hand: a device attached to the end of a manipulator arm having a mechanism with closing jaws or other means to grasp objects.

hard automation: a production method in which equipment has specifically been engineered for a unique manufacturing sequence. "Hard" automation suggests programming with hardware in contrast to "soft" automation, which uses software or computer programming.

hardware: the electronic and mechanical structure of a computer or a robot controller.

hardware debugging: the method of finding and fixing malfunctioning electronic equipment, particularly digital equipment.

hardwired (hard-wired): pertaining to a physical connection or characteristic; for example, the address of a console or I/O device.

HARPY: a simple experimental speech-understanding system intended to show what can be done without resorting to sophisticated methods.

hash total: the result obtained by applying an algorithm to a set of data for checking purposes; for example, a sum of the numerical values of specified data items. synonymous with *control total*.

HC: see *host computer*.

HD: see *half-duplex*.

HDLC: see *high-level data-link control*.

HDX: see *half-duplex*.

head (H): a device that reads, writes, or erases data on a storage medium; for example, a small electromagnet used to read, write, or erase data on a magnetic drum or magnetic tape, or the set of perforating, reading, or marking devices used for punching, reading, or printing on perforated tape.

header card: a card that contains information related to the data in cards that follow.

HEARSAY architecture: synonymous with *blackboard architecture*.

HEARSAY II: a sophisticated experimental speech-understanding system stressing the importance of multiple specialized methods and complicated approaches for procedure interaction.

HELP: a robot language which can control multiple Cartesian arms in assembly tasks.

heuristic: pertaining to exploratory methods of problem solving in which solutions are discovered by evaluation of the progress made toward the final result. cf. *algorithm*.

heuristic knowledge: synonymous with *experiential knowledge*.

heuristic problem solving: the ability to plan and direct actions to achieve higher-order objectives.

heuristic rules: rules written to capture the heuristics an expert uses for solving a problem. The expert's original heuristics may not have taken the form of *if-then* rules, and one of the problems involved in building a knowledge system is converting an expert's heuristic knowledge into rules. The power of a knowledge system reflects the heuristic rules in the knowledge base.

heuristic search: a problem-solving technique for determining a sequence of operators that transforms an initial state into a desired goal state.

hexadecimal: synonymous with *sexadecimal*.

hexadecimal numbering system: a base 16 number system commonly used when printing the contents of main memory to aid programmers in detecting errors.

hidden lines: line segments that are not visible to the viewer of a three-dimensional displayed object because they are behind other surfaces of the object.

hierarchical control: a distributed control method in which the controlling processes are arranged in a hierarchy.

hierarchy: a relationship of elements in a structure divided into levels, with those at higher levels having priority or precedence over those at lower levels. see *control hierarchy; sensory hierarchy.*

hierarchy, input, process, output: see *HIPO.*

high-level data link control (HDLC): the control of data links by use of a specified series of bits rather than by the control characters of the ISO standard 7-bit character set for information processing interchange.

high-level language (HLL)

(1) a programming language that does not reflect the structure of any one given computer or that of any given class of computers.

(2) a problem-oriented language that requires little knowledge of the computer on which a program written in the language is to be run; this facilitates translation of computer programs in this language into several different machine codes. This capability usually results in many machine instructions for each statement in the source program (e.g., ALGOL, COBOL, COGO, FORTRAN, PL/1, SIMSCRIPT).

high-order position: the left-most position in a string of characters.

HIPO: Hierarchy, Input, Process, Output. A graphics tool for designing, developing, and documenting program function.

HLL: see *high-level language.*

Hollerith card: a punch card characterized by 80 columns and 12 rows of punch positions. see also *punched card.*

holography: three-dimensional pictures produced by laser beams.

horn clause: in logic programming, expressions connected by "or," with at most one positive proposition; taking the form "not *A* or not *B* or not *C* or *D*, and so on." Logical programming is made more efficient by restricting the type of logical assertions to horn clauses in ways similar where production systems insist on having knowledge stated in terms of *if-then* rules.

81

host computer (HC)
(1)   in a network, a computer that primarily provides services such as computation, data base access, or special programs or programming languages.
(2)   the primary or controlling computer in a multiple computer installation.
(3)   a computer used to prepare programs for use on another computer or on another data processing system; for example, a computer used to compile, link, edit, or test programs to be used on another system.
(4)   synonymous with *host processor*.

host processor: synonymous with *host computer*.

housekeeping operation: an operation that facilitates the execution of a computer program without making a direct contribution. For example, initialization of storage areas or the execution of a calling sequence. synonymous with *overhead operation*.

HS: see *half-subtractor*.

human information processing: an interpretation of human thinking that is influenced by how computers work; focuses on the information that an individual uses to reach a conclusion, and then asks how one could design a computer program that would begin with that same information and reach that same conclusion.

human interface: one subsystem of an expert system, or any computing system, with which the human user deals routinely. It aims to be as natural as possible, employing language as close as possible to ordinary language (or the stylized language of a given field) and understanding and displaying images, all at speeds that are comfortable and natural for humans. see also *knowledge base management system*.

humanoid: a robot that physically resembles a human being.

hybrid system building tools: see *large, hybrid system building tools*.

hydraulic: the use of water or oil in tubes to transmit power from one location to another.

hydraulic motor: an actuator with interconnected units that convert high-pressure hydraulic or pneumatic fluid into mechanical rotation or shaft movement.

hydraulic robot: a robot having a hydraulic power supply as either a separate unit or an integral section; contains an electric motor-driven pump, filter, reservoir, and often a heat exchanger.

82

hypothetical worlds: a means of structuring knowledge in a knowledge-based system for defining the contexts (hypothetical worlds) in which facts and rules apply.

hysteresis: the lagging of a physical response of a body behind its cause. The asymmetry between the force/displacement relationship in one direction and that of another direction.

I

I: see *input.*

IAR: see *instruction address register.*

IC: see *integrated circuit.*

ICAI: Intelligent Computer-Aided Instruction. Instructional software that incorporates AI techniques. Requires the development of methods that allow the system to monitor an individual student's responses and develop a model of how the student conceptualizes the situation. Then, based on such a user model, the system varies its presentation to systematically develop the size and accuracy of the student's cognitive model of the subject. synonymous with *intelligent tutoring systems.*

ICAM: Integrated Computer-Aided Manufacturing. A U.S. Air Force project established to automate production within the aircraft industry.

ICU: see *instruction control unit.*

ID: see *identifier.*

identifier (ID): a character or group of characters used to identify or name items of data, and possibly to indicate certain properties of that data.

identity element: a logic element that performs an identity operation. synonymous with *identity gate.*

identity gate: synonymous with *identity element.*

identity operation: the boolean operation the result of which has the boolean value 1, if and only if all the operands have the same boolean value. An identity operation on two operands is an equivalence operation. cf. *nonidentity operation.*

IDP: see *integrated data processing.*

I/F: see *interface.*

IF-AND-ONLY-IF element: a logic element that performs the boolean operation of equivalence. synonymous with *IF-AND-ONLY-IF gate.*

IF-AND-ONLY-IF gate: synonymous with *IF-AND-ONLY-IF element.*

IF-AND-ONLY-IF operation: synonymous with *equivalence operation.*

IF-THEN element: a logic element that performs the boolean operation of implication. synonymous with *IF-THEN gate.*

IF-THEN gate: synonymous with *IF-THEN element.*

if-then rule: a statement of the relationship among a set of facts. The relationships may be definitional (e.g., if female and married, then wife), or heuristic (e.g., if cloudy, then take an umbrella).

illegal character: a character or combination of bits that is not valid according to some criteria; for example, with respect to a specified alphabet, a character that is not a member.

image processing: processing of images using computer techniques.

image understanding: using artificial intelligence techniques for processing and interpreting visual images (e.g., analyzing the signals produced by a television camera to recognize and classify the types of objects in the picture).

immediate-access storage: a storage device whose access time is negligible in comparison with other operating times.

immediate address: the contents of an address part that contains the value of an operand rather than an address. synonymous *with zero-level address.*

immediate instruction: an instruction that contains an operand for the operation specified, rather than simply an address of the operand.

impact printer (IP): a printer in which printing is the result of mechanical impacts.

implementation

(1) the overall environment in which an expert system functions; includes the hardware the system will run on, the operating system that will support the expert system, any higher-level languages that the system will depend on, and any interfaces that the system will have with other computer systems or sensors. synonymous with *implementation environment.*

(2) the sixth phase in knowledge engineering, this involves actually fielding the system. This can involve porting the system to different hardware, and involves training user personnel to accept and use the new system. For other phases see *knowledge engineering.*

implementation environment: synonymous with *implementation.*

implicator: the dyadic boolean operation the result of which has the boolean value 0 if and only if the first operand has the boolean value 0 and the second has the boolean value 1.

IN: see *input.*

inclusive-OR element: a logic element that performs the boolean operation of disjunction. synonymous with *inclusive-OR gate.*

inclusive-OR gate: synonymous with *inclusive-OR element.*

inclusive-OR operation: synonymous with *disjunction.*

incremental computer

(1) a computer that represents as absolute values the changes to variables, instead of the variables themselves.

(2) a computer in which incremental representation of data is mainly used.

incremental integrator: a digital integrator modified so that the output signal is maximum negative, zero, or maximum positive when the value of the input is negative, zero, or positive, respectively.

incremental learning: a multistage learning process in which information already learned at one stage is adopted to accommodate new facts provided in future stages.

IND: see *indicator.*

index

(1) in programming, a subscript of integer value that identifies the position of an item of data with respect to some other item of data.

(2) a list of the contents of a file or of a document, together with keys or references for locating the contents.

(3) a symbol or a numeral used to identify a particular quantity in an array of similar quantities. For example, the terms of an array represented by X1, X2, . . .X100 have the indexes 1, 2, . . .100, respectively.

(4) to move a machine part to a predetermined position, or by a predetermined amount, on a quantized scale.

(5) a table used to locate the records of an indexed sequential data set.

indexed address: an address that is modified by the content of an index register prior to or during the execution of a computer instruction.

indexed sequential file: a sequential file ordered on the basis of unique record keys having index stored housing addresses or pointers to show where each record in the file is located; stored on a direct access storage unit and accessed sequentially or randomly.

indexing: a technique of address modification using index registers.

index register (IX): a register whose contents may be used to modify an operand address during the execution of computer instructions; it can also be used as a counter. May be used to control the execution of a loop, to control the use of an array, as a switch for table lookup, or as a pointer.

index word: an index modifier applied to the address part of a computer instruction.

indicator (IND)

(1)   a device that may be set into a prescribed state, usually according to the result of a previous process or on the occurrence of a specified condition in the equipment, and that usually gives a visual or other indication of the existence of the prescribed state. It may also be used, in some cases, to determine the selection among alternative processes; for example, an overflow indicator.

(2)   an item of data that may be interrogated to determine whether a particular condition has been satisfied in the execution of a computer program; for example, a switch indicator, an overflow indicator. see also *flag*.

indirect address: an address that designates the storage location of an item of data to be treated as the address of an operand, but not necessarily as its direct address. synonymous with *multilevel address*.

induction motor: an alternating current motor producing torque when a rotating magnetic field meets electric current inducted in circuits or coils.

induction system: a knowledge system having a knowledge base consisting of examples. An induction algorithm builds a decision tree from the examples, and the system goes on to deliver advice. These systems do not facilitate the development of hierarchies of rules. synonymous with *example-driven system*.

inductive inference: a mode of reasoning starting with given facts and concluding with general hypotheses or theories from which initial acts are rederived via deductive inference. see also *deductive inference*. cf. *inductive learning*.

inductive learning: learning by generalizing facts and observations obtained from a teacher or environment. cf. *inductive inference*.

industrial robot: a reprogrammable, multifunctional manipulator designed to move material, parts, tools, or specialized devices through variable programmed motions for the performance of a variety of tasks.

industrial robot components: the principal units of an industrial robot, which are (1) one or more arms, usually situated on a fixed base, that move in several directions; (2) a manipulator (the "hand" for holding the tool or the part to be worked on); and (3) a controller providing detailed movement instructions.

inference: a process by which new facts are derived from known facts. A rule (e.g., if the sky is black, then the time is night), combined with a rule of inference (e.g., modus ponens) and a known fact (e.g., the sky is black), results in a new fact (e.g., the time is night).

inference, data-directed: an inference that is driven by events rather than goals. see also *forward chaining.*

inference, goal-directed: an inference that is driven by goals rather than data. see also *backward chaining.*

inference chain: the sequence of steps or rule applications utilized by a rule-based system to reach a conclusion.

inference engine: that portion of a knowledge system containing the inference and control strategies; includes various knowledge acquisition, explanation, and user interface subsystems. Inference engines are characterized by the inference and control strategies they use; for example, the inference engine of MYCIN uses modus ponens and backward chaining.

inference method: a technique utilized by the inference engine for accessing and applying the domain knowledge; for example, backward chaining and forward chaining.

inference net: all possible inference chains generated from the rules in a rule-based system.

inference rule: a rule concluding new facts from old ones, either by the application of strict logical principles or more imperfect, plausible methods. see also *deductive inference; inductive inference.*

inference system: see *symbolic inference.*

infix notation: a method of forming mathematical expressions, governed by rules of operator precedence and using parentheses, in which the operators are dispersed among the operands, each operator indicating the operation to be performed on the operands or the intermediate results adjacent to it. cf. *prefix notation.*

information bits: in data communication, those bits that are generated by the data source and which are not used for error control by the data transmission system.

information content binary unit: see *Shannon.*

information separator (IS):   any control character used to delimit like units of data in a hierarchic arrangement of data. The name of the separator does not necessarily indicate the units of data it separates. synonymous with *separating character.*

information storage and retrieval (IS&R): utilizing a computer system for storing significant amounts of related data, items of which can rapidly and easily be retrieved and viewed.

inheritance: a process by which characteristics of one object are assumed to be characteristics of another; for example, if we determine that an animal is a bird, then we automatically assume that the animal has all of the characteristics of birds.

inheritance hierarchies: when knowledge is represented in a hierarchy, the characteristics of superordinate objects are inherited by subordinate objects. Thus, if we determine that an auto loan is a type of loan, then we know that the credit check procedures that apply to all loans apply to auto loans.

INIT: see *initialize.*

initialize (INIT): to set counters, switches, addresses, or contents of storage to zero or other starting values at the beginning of, or at prescribed points in, the operation of a computer routine.

initial program loader (IPL): the utility routine that loads the initial part of a computer program (such as an operating system or other computer program) so that the computer program can then proceed under its own control. cf. *bootstrap.*

in-line procedure: in COBOL, the set of statements that constitutes the main or controlling flow of the computer program and which excludes statements executed under control of the asynchronous control system.

in-line processing: the processing of data in random order, not subject to preliminary editing or sorting.

INP: see *input.*

input (I) (IN) (INP)

(1)   one, or a sequence of, input states.

(2)   pertaining to a device process or channel involved in an input process, or to the data or states involved in an input process. In the English language, the adjective input may be used in place of such terms as input data, input signal, and input terminal, when such usage is clear in a given context.

(3)   synonymous with *input data; input process.*

input channel: a channel for impressing a state on a device or logic element.

input data: synonymous with *input*.

input/output (I/O)

(1) pertaining to either input or output signals or both.

(2) equipment used to communicate with a computer.

(3) data used in communications with a computer.

(4) the media carrying the data for input/output.

input/output channel: synonymous with *data channel*.

input/output controller (IOC): a functional unit in an automatic data processing system that controls one or more units of peripheral equipment. synonymous with *I/O controller; peripheral control unit*.

input/output port: a connection to a computer for transmitting data to or from the computer.

input/output system: hardware and software required to enter data into a computer and to transfer it between various input/output devices and main memory.

input/output unit (IOU): a device in a data processing system by which data may be entered into the system, received from the system, or both.

input process: synonymous with *input*.

input signals: electric signals possessing the presence or absence of a specific voltage at the input signal terminals for telling the robot when or where not to do something. This application can bring out the cost effectiveness of a computer-controlled robot, because additional switching logic hardware is not needed.

inquiry station

(1) a user terminal primarily for the interrogation of an automatic data processing system.

(2) data terminal equipment for inquiry into a data processing system.

INST: see *instruction*.

installation: the process of connecting the hardware in a computer system, and the specific hardware making up the computer system; for example, one installation can be a processor, keyboard, monitor, and disk drive.

instantiation: the specification of particular values. A specific person with a specific sex and temperature is an instantiation of the generic object "patient."

INSTR: see *instruction*.

instruction (INST) (INSTR): in a programming language, a meaningful expression that specifies one operation and identifies its operands, if any.

instruction address

(1) the address of an instruction.

(2) the address that must be used to fetch an instruction.

instruction address register (IAR): a register from whose contents the address of the next instruction is derived. An instruction address register may also be a portion of a storage device specifically designated for the derivation of the address of the next instruction by a translator, compiler, interpreter, language processor, operating system, and so on. synonymous with *control counter; sequence control register.*

instructional software: computer software used either for instruction or for aiding the actual performance of a task.

instruction control unit (ICU): in a processing unit, the part that receives instructions in proper sequence, interprets each instruction, and applies the proper signals to the arithmetic and logic unit and other parts in accordance with this interpretation.

instruction cycle: a sequence of events in which an instruction is searched, decoded, and executed.

instruction register (IR): a register that is used to hold an instruction for interpretation.

instruction set: the set of instructions of a computer, a programming language, or the programming languages in a programming system.

instruction word: a word that represents an instruction.

INT: see *interrupt.*

integer programming: in operations research, a class of procedures for locating the maximum or minimum of a function subject constraints, where some or all variables must have integer values. synonymous with *discrete programming.*

integral control: a control method whereby the signal that drives the actuator equals the time integral of the difference between the input (desired output) and the measured actual output.

integrated circuit (IC): a combination of interconnected circuit elements inseparably associated on or within a continuous substrate.

Integrated Computer-Aided Manufacturing: see *ICAM.*

integrated data processing (IDP): data processing in which the coordination of data acquisition and other stages of data processing are combined in a coherent data processing system.

integrated system: synonymous with *total systems.*

integrator

(1)   a device whose output variable is the integral of the input variable with respect to time.

(2)   a device whose output function is proportional to the integral of the input function with respect to a specified variable; for example, a watt-hour meter.

INTELLECT: the first commercially successful natural language interface.

intelligent assistants: synonymous with *expert system.*

intelligent computer-aided instruction: see *ICAI.*

intelligent robot: a robot that can be programmed to make performance choices contingent on sensory inputs.

intelligent terminal: a communication station containing storage and some of the components of a small computer, and which permits batch data to be organized and edited before being transmitted to a central computer.

intelligent tutoring systems: synonymous with *ICAI.*

intelligent work station: synonymous with *work station.*

interactive multiprocessing environment: a set of software that is readily accessed and used.

interactive routine: a programming routine where a series of operations is repeatedly performed, until an earlier specified end condition is reached.

interactive system: a computer system where the user communicates directly and rapidly with the central processor through a terminal.

interconnection: signals received by a robot so that it can interface to a working environment; for example, limit-switch signals to the robot when a part is in position.

interface (I/F)

(1)   a shared boundary. An interface might be a hardware component to link two devices, or it might be a portion of storage or registers accessed by two or more computer programs.

(2)   a common boundary between two systems or pieces of equipment where they are joined.

(3)   the link between a computer program and the outside environment. Knowledge systems have interfaces for development (the knowl-

93

edge acquisition interface) and for users (the user interface). Some systems have interfaces that pass information to and from other programs, data bases, display devices, or sensors.

INTERLISP: a dialect of LISP. A programming environment that provides a programmer with many aids to facilitate the development and maintenance of large LISP programs. see also *list processing*.

interlock: to prevent a machine or device from initiating further operations until the operation in process is completed.

internal sensor: a sensor that measures displacements, forces, or other variables internal to the robot.

internal sort

(1)   a sort performed within internal storage.

(2)   a sort program or sort phase that sorts two or more items within main storage.

(3)   a sorting technique that creates sequences of records or keys. Usually, it is a prelude to a merge phase in which the sequences created are reduced to one by an external merge.

internal storage: storage that is accessible by a computer without the use of input/output channels. synonymous with *primary storage unit; processor storage*.

intern(ed): in LISP, a technique in a package in which it is accessible in the package and is owned by the package, or by another package from which it can be accessed. Also, where the LISP reader can find the symbol in a package when it is interned, and cannot find the symbol in a package when it is uninterned.

INTERNIST: see *CADUCEUS*.

interoceptor: an internal sensor, usually used in physiology.

INTERP: see *interpreter*.

interpolator: a computer algorithm or hardware circuit that inserts intermediate points between two given end points of a segment or trajectory, and emits reference commands to the control loops in order to coordinate their motion to obtain a required path such as a straight line or a circle.

interpret: to translate and to execute each source language statement of a computer program before translating and executing the next statement.

interpreter (INTERP)
(1)   a computer program used to interpret. synonymous with *interpretive program.*
(2)   in punched card operations, a device that prints characters corresponding to hole patterns punched in the card.
interpretive language: a programming language needing the support of an interpreter during execution. see *interpreter.*
interpretive program: synonymous with *interpreter (1).*
interrecord gap (IRG)
(1)   a machine-generated space on magnetic tape appearing after each data block.
(2)   an area on a data medium that signals the end of a block or record.
interrupt (INT) (INTR)
(1)   a suspension of a process such as the execution of a computer program caused by an event external to that process, and performed in such a way that the process can be resumed.
(2)   to stop a process in such a way that it can be resumed.
(3)   in data transmission, to take an action at a receiving station that causes the transmitting station to terminate a transmission.
(4)   synonymous with *interruption.*
interruption: synonymous with *interrupt.*
intersection: synonymous with *conjunction.*
INTR: see *interrupt.*
inverted file
(1)   a file whose sequence has been reversed.
(2)   in information retrieval, a method of organizing a cross-index file in which a key word identifies a record; the items, numbers, or documents pertinent to that key word are indicated.
I/O: input/output.
IOC: see *input/output controller.*
I/O controller: synonymous with *input/output controller.*
IOU: see *input/output unit.*
IP: see *impact printer.*
IPL: see *initial program loader.*
IR: see *instruction register.*
IRG: see *interrecord gap.*
IS&R: see *information storage and retrieval.*

item

(1)   one member of a group. A file may consist of a number of items, such as records, which in turn may consist of other items.

(2)   a collection of related characters, treated as a unit.

IX: see *index register*.

J

JCS: see *job control statement.*

jig: a unit for holding and locating a workpiece that also guides, controls, or limits one or more cutting tools.

JIRA: Japanese Industrial Robot Association. The first in the world, formed in 1971.

job

(1) a set of data that completely defines a unit of work for a computer. A job usually includes all necessary computer programs, linkages, files, and instructions to the operating system.

(2) a collection of related problem programs, identified in the input stream by a JOB statement followed by one or more EXEC and DO statements.

job aids: devices that aid individuals when they perform tasks. Well-constructed job aids permit a performer to avoid memorization by allowing individuals to perform jobs more rapidly and more accurately than they would if they had been trained in any conventional fashion. Since performers memorize frequently used responses while using job aids, these aids serve as structured on-the-job training. synonymous with *performance aids.*

job control statement (JCS): a statement in a job that is used in identifying the job or describing its requirements to the operating system.

job shop: a discrete parts manufacturing facility characterized by a mix of products of relatively low-volume production in batch lots.

joint: the junction of two member links of the robot manipulator where the members can move freely.

jointed-arm robot: a robot having rotary joints in several places along the arm, corresponding to a person's shoulder, elbow, and wrist.

jointed-spherical robot: see *jointed-arm robot.*

joint space: the vector that specifies the angular or translational displacement of each joint of a multidegree-of-freedom linkage relative to a reference displacement for each such joint.

joystick: a movable handle that a person grasps and rotates to a limited extent in one or more degrees of freedom and whose variable position or applied force is measured, resulting in commands to a control system.

jump: synonymous with *branch*.

K

K: when referring to storage capacity, 2 to the 10th power; 1024 in decimal notation.

Karnaugh map: a rectangular diagram of a logic function of variables drawn with overlapping rectangles representing a unique combination of the logic variables, and such that an intersection is shown for all combinations. see also *map*.

KB: see *keyboard*.

KBD: see *keyboard*.

K-byte: see *kilobyte*.

KEE: a tool for assembling knowledge bases for expert systems.

key

(1) one or more characters within a set of data that contain information about the set, including its identification.

(2) in sorting, synonym for *control word*.

(3) in COBOL, one or more data items, the contents of which identify the type or location of a record, or the ordering of data.

(4) to enter information from a keyboard.

KEYBD: see *keyboard*.

keyboard (KB) (KBD) (KEYBD)

(1) a systematic arrangement of keys by which a machine is operated or by which data is entered.

(2) a device for the encoding of data by key depression which causes the generation of the selected code element.

(3) a group of numeric keys, alphabetic keys, or function keys used for entering information into a terminal and into the system.

kilobyte (K-byte): the number of bytes given by 2 raised to the 10th power.

KIPS: see *Knowledge Information Processing Systems*.

knowledge: an integrated collection of facts and relationships which, when exercised, produces competent performance. The quantity and quality of knowledge possessed by an individual or a computer can be judged by the variety of situations in which the individual or program obtains successful results.

knowledge acquisition: the process of locating, collecting, and refining knowledge; may require interviews with experts, research in a library, or introspection. The individual doing this must convert the acquired knowledge into a form that can be used by a computer program. synonymous with *expertise acquisition.*

knowledge base: facts, assumptions, beliefs, heuristics, and expertise; methods of dealing with the data base to achieve desired results such as a diagnosis, interpretation, or solution to a problem.

knowledge base management system: one of the subsystems in an expert system. This subsystem manages the knowledge base by automatically organizing, controlling, propagating, and updating stored knowledge. It initiates searches for knowledge relevant to the line of reasoning upon which the inference subsystem is working. see also *human interface.*

knowledge compilation: translating learning concerned with transferring knowledge from humans or a task environment into computers. synonymous with *operationalization.*

knowledge engineer: an individual whose specialty is assessing problems, acquiring knowledge, and building knowledge systems.

knowledge engineering: the art of designing and building expert systems and other knowledge-based programs. For a definition of the seven phases in developing a small expert system see, in sequence: *front end analysis; task analysis; prototype development; system development; field testing; implementation;* and *maintenance.*

Knowledge Information Processing Systems (KIPS): the new, fifth generation of computers that the Japanese propose to build which will have symbolic inference capabilities, coupled with very large knowledge bases and superb human interfaces, all combined with high processing speeds, so that the machines will greatly amplify human intellectual capabilities.

knowledge representation: a means for encoding and storing facts and relationships in a knowledge base. Semantic networks, object-attribute-value triplets, production rules, frames, and logical expressions are all ways to represent knowledge.

knowledge source: a collection of rules, procedures, and/or data for solving problems of a very specific nature. It is larger than a rule but smaller than an expert system (e.g., in blackboard architectures, each process that has access to the shared memory).

knowledge system: a computer program using knowledge and inference procedures to solve difficult problems. The knowledge needed to perform at such a level, plus the inference procedures used, can be thought of as a model of the expertise of skilled practitioners. In contrast to expert systems, knowledge systems are designed to solve small, difficult problems rather than large problems requiring true human expertise. see also *expert system*.

L

L: see *language*.

ladder diagram: an electrical engineering method for schematically illustrating functions in an electrical circuit (relays, switches, times, etc.) by diagramming them in a vertical sequence resembling a ladder.

lag

(1) the delay between two events.

(2) the time it takes a signal or an object to move from one location to another.

language (L): a set of characters, conventions, and rules that is used for conveying information. The three aspects of language are pragmatics, semantics, and syntax.

language processor: a computer program that performs such functions as translating, interpreting, and other tasks required for processing a specified programming language.

language–tool spectrum: a continuum along which various software products are placed. At one extreme are narrowly defined tools that are optimized to perform specific tasks. At the other extreme are general purpose languages used for many different applications.

language translator: a general term for any assembler, compiler, or other routine that accepts statements in one language and produces equivalent statements in another language.

large, hybrid system building tools: a class of knowledge engineering tools that emphasizes flexibility; designed for building large knowledge bases. They include a hybrid collection of different inference and control strategies. Most commercial hybrid tools incorporate frames and facilitate object-oriented programming.

large, narrow system building tools: a class of knowledge engineering tools that sacrifices flexibility to facilitate the efficient development of more narrowly defined expert systems.

large scale integration (LSI): the process of integrating large numbers of circuits on a single chip of semiconductor material.

laser: a straight beam of light made up of highly concentrated molecules.

latch register: a register that can capture data and hold it.

latency: the time interval between the instant at which an instruction control unit initiates a call for data and the instant at which the actual transfer of the data is started. synonymous with *waiting time; wait state.*

LCB: see *line control block.*

lead through: programming or teaching by physically guiding the robot through the desired actions. The speed of the robot is increased when programming is complete. see also *programming.*

learning: a change in the system altering its long-term performance. In production systems, it can be effected by the automatic addition, deletion, or modification of rules.

learning by being told: synonymous with *learning from instructions.*

learning control: a control method wherein experience is automatically used to provide for future control decisions, which will be better than those in the past.

learning from examples: a form of inductive learning that infers a general concept description from examples and (optionally) counterexamples of that concept.

learning from instructions: transforming and integrating instructions from an external source into an internally usable form. synonymous with *advice taking; learning by being told.*

learning from observation: constructing descriptions, hypotheses, or theories about a given collection of facts or observations, with no a priori classification of observations into sets exemplifying wanted concepts. synonymous with *learning without a teacher; unsupervised learning.*

learning without a teacher: synonymous with *learning from observation.*

LED: see *light-emitting diode.*

left-hand side (LHS): one of the two parts of a rule, specifying the antecedents that must be satisfied if the rule is to be applied. see also *right-hand side.*

left memory: a data structure in the Rete match algorithm network associated with a node and containing the combinations of working memory elements and variable bindings that constitute a consistent match for the condition element being tested at the node and all preceding condition elements.

level: the degree of subordination of an item in a hierarchic arrangement.

level of automation: the degree to which a process has been made automatic.

lexical-free variables: in LISP, a value found in one environment, but not found in several environments. cf. *dynamic-free variables.*

lexical scoping: in LISP, free variables scoped when they are closed at definition time; that is, the time a variable is used in a function.

lexicon: the morphemes of a language, or the words used within a subject area.

LHS: see *left-hand side.*

library

(1) a collection of related files. For example, one line of an invoice may form an item, a complete invoice may form a file, the collection of inventory control files may form a library, and the libraries used by an organization are known as its data bank.

(2) a repository for demountable recorded media such as magnetic disk packs and magnetic tapes.

life: a self-organizing and self-replicating system.

light-emitting diode (LED): a semiconductor unit giving off light when current passes through it.

limited-degree-of-freedom robot: a robot able to position and orient its end effector in fewer than six degrees of freedom.

limit switch: an electrical switch positioned to be actuated when a specific motion limit occurs, thereby deactivating the actuator causing that motion.

line (LN)

(1) on a terminal, one or more characters entered before a return to the first printing or display position.

(2) a string of characters accepted by the system as a single block of input from a terminal; for example, all characters entered before a carriage return or all characters entered before the terminal user hits the attention key.

linear-array camera: a TV camera, usually solid; state, with an aspect ratio of 1:*n* today, *n* is typically 128, 256, or 512.

linear interpolation: a function automatically performed in the control that defines the continuum of points in a straight line based on only two taught coordinate positions. All calculated points are automatically inserted between the taught coordinate positions upon playback.

linearity

(1) a constant ratio of incremental cause and effect.

(2) the degree to which an input/output relationship is proportional.

(3) the degree to which a motion intended to be in a straight line conforms to a straight line.

linear language: a language that is customarily expressed as a linear representation; for example, FORTRAN is a linear language, a flow-chart is not.

linear optimization: synonymous with *linear programming*.

linear programming: in operations research, a procedure for locating the maximum or minimum of a linear function of variables that is subject to linear constraints. synonymous with *linear optimization*. cf. *convex programming; dynamic programming; nonlinear programming*.

linear test and merge: an algorithm employing a directed acyclic graph, performing sequences of tests along chains of directed arcs, and merging results of tests at nodes where two or more chains interact.

line-at-a-time printer: synonymous with *line printer*.

line control block (LCB): a storage area containing control information required for scheduling and managing line operations. One LCB is maintained for each line.

line control discipline: synonymous with *protocol*.

line discipline: synonymous with *protocol*.

line of sight: a line from a vision sensor attached to a robot's end effector to a distant point toward which the robot must move.

line printer (LP) (LPT): a device that prints a line of characters as a unit. synonymous with *line-at-a-time printer*.

link

(1) the part of a computer program—in some cases, a single instruction or an address—that passes control and parameters between separate portions of the computer program. synonymous with *linkage*.

(2) to provide a link. see also *data link*.

106

(3) in robotics, a connecting element in the robot manipulator.

linkage: synonymous with *link*.

LISP: see *list processing*. see also *LOGO*.

LISP object: a data structure that can be any of several things: number, vector, symbol, list, function, or macro, depending mostly on its representation in memory.

LISP printer: see *LISP reader*.

LISP program: a list containing a function that contains other functions, atoms, or lists as arguments.

LISP reader: related to the printer, to objects, and to the print names of objects. Accepts a stream of characters as input, interprets the characters as the representation of an object, builds the object in memory, and returns the object, ostensibly to know that the process is completed.

LISP symbol: a data object having the following components: a property list providing a symbol with modifiable, named components; a name used for identifying the symbol (print name); and a package cell used for locating a symbol, when given its name.

list

(1) an ordered set of items of data.

(2) to print or otherwise display items.

(3) in LISP, a collection of elements within parentheses; for example, atoms, functions, or other lists.

(4) in LISP, the function which accepts two lists as arguments and returns them as elements of a list.

(5) see *push-down list; push-up list*.

list processing (LISP): a method of processing data in the form of lists. Usually, chained lists are used so that the logical order of items can be changed without altering their physical locations.

list structure: a collection of items enclosed by parentheses, where each item is either a symbol or another list.

LN: see *line*.

load

(1) in programming, to enter data into storage or working registers.

(2) to bring a load module from auxiliary storage into main storage for execution.

(3) to put a magnetic tape onto a tape drive or to put cards into a card reader.

load-and-go: an operating technique in which there are no stops between the loading and executing phases of a computer program, and which may include assembling or compiling.

load capacity: the maximum weight or mass of a material that is handled by a machine or process without failure.

load deflection

(1) the difference in position of some point on a body between a nonloaded and an externally loaded condition.

(2) the difference in position of a manipulator hand or tool, usually with the arm extended, between a nonloaded condition and an externally loaded condition. Either or both static and dynamic loads can be considered.

local variable: in LISP, an identifiable variable when the scope of the value of a variable is limited to the code that gets evaluated during a call to a function. Local variables have no corresponding data structures, packages, or property lists.

locating surfaces: machined surfaces on a part used as reference surfaces for precise locating and clamping of the part in a fixture.

locomotion: some means of moving around in a specified environment.

logger

(1) a functional unit that records events and physical conditions, usually with respect to time.

(2) a device that enables a user entity to log in; for example, to identify itself, its purpose, and the time of entry, and to log out with the corresponding data so that the appropriate accounting procedures may be carried out in accordance with the operating system.

logic: a system prescribing rules for manipulating symbols. Common systems of logic powerful enough to deal with knowledge structures include propositional calculus and predicate calculus.

logical ADD: synonymous with *disjunction*.

logical comparison: a logic operation used to determine if two strings are identical.

logical expression

(1) an expression that contains logical operators and operands, and that can be reduced to a value that is true or false.

(2) in assembler programming, a conditional assembly expression that is a combination of logical terms, logical operators, and paired parentheses.

108

(3)   in FORTRAN, a combination of logical primaries and logical operators.

logical multiply: synonymous with *AND*.

logical operations: nonarithmetic operations such as selecting, sorting, matching, comparing, and so on.

logical product: synonymous with *conjunction*.

logical record (LR)

(1)   a record independent of its physical environment. Portions of the same logical record may be located in different physical records, or several logical records or parts of logical records may be located in one physical record.

(2)   a record from a standpoint of its content, function, and use rather than its physical attributes; that is, one that is defined in terms of the information it contains.

(3)   in COBOL, the most inclusive data item, identified by a level-01 entry. It consists of one or more related data items.

logical shift: a shift that equally affects all of the characters of a computer word. synonymous with *logic shift*.

logic-based methods: programming techniques using predicate calculus to structure the program and guide execution.

logic elements: various forms of electrical switches within a computer. synonymous with *switching elements*.

logic shift: synonymous with *logical shift*.

LOGO: a popular computer language derived from LISP that supports turtle graphics.

long-term memory: a portion of human memory that is exceedingly large and contains all of the information that is not currently being processed.

long-term repeatability: the closeness of agreement of position movements, repeated under the same conditions during a long time interval, to the same location.

loop

(1)   a set of instructions that may be executed repeatedly while a certain condition prevails. In some implementations, no test is made to discover whether the condition prevails until the loop has been executed once.

(2)   in data communication, an electrical path connection, that is, a station and a channel.

low-order position: the rightmost position in a string of characters.

LP: see *line printer.*

LPT: see *line printer.*

LR: see *logical record.*

LSI: see *large scale integration.*

Lukasiewics notation: synonymous with *prefix notation.*

M

M
(1) see *mantissa*.
(2) see *mega*.
(3) see *memory*.
(4) see *modem*.

machine address: synonymous with *absolute address*.

machine cycle
(1) the identified time interval in which a computer can perform a given number of operations.
(2) the shortest complete process of action that is repeated in order.
(3) the minimum amount of time in which the preceding can be performed.

machine language (ML)
(1) a language that is used directly by a machine.
(2) instructions written in a form that is intelligible to the internal circuitry of the computer; written in binary code, using 1's and 0's. synonymous with *computer language*.

machine learning: a research activity seeking to create computer programs that can learn from experience. see also *learning*.

machine logic
(1) built-in methods of problem approach and function execution; the way a system is designed to perform, what its activities are, and the type and form of data it can utilize internally.
(2) the capability of an automatic data processing unit to make decisions based upon the results of tests performed.

machine word: synonymous with *computer word*.

MacLISP: a dialect of LISP that is tuned for efficiency, but less friendly as a developmental environment. see also *list processing*.

macro: programming with instructions in a source language.

macrocall: synonymous with *macro instruction*.

macrodefinition: see *macro instruction.*

macrogenerating program: synonymous with *macrogenerator.*

macrogenerator: a computer program that replaces macroinstructions in the source language with the defined sequence of instructions in the source language. synonymous with *macrogenerating program.*

macroinstruction

(1) an instruction in a source language that is to be replaced by a defined sequence of instructions in the same source language. The macroinstruction may also specify values for parameters in the instructions that are to replace it.

(2) in assembler programming, an assembler-language statement that causes the assembler to process a predefined set of statements called a *macrodefinition.* The statements normally produced from the macroinstruction replace the macroinstruction in the program. synonymous with *macrocall.*

macrooperator: an operator composed of a sequence of more primitive operators that simplify problem solving by permitting a more coarse grain problem-solving search.

MACSYMA: a large computer system with procedures for aiding people to do complicated applied mathematics.

magnetic card (MC): a card with a magnetizable surface layer on which data can be stored by magnetic recording.

magnetic core

(1) a piece of magnetic material, usually toroidal in shape, used for storage.

(2) a configuration of magnetic material that is, or is intended to be, placed in a spatial relationship to current-carrying conductors and whose magnetic properties are essential to its use. It may be used to concentrate an induced magnetic field, as in a transformer induction coil or armature, to retain a magnetic polarization for the purpose of storing data, or, for its nonlinear properties (as in a logic element). It may be made of iron, iron oxide, or ferrite and occur in such shapes as wires, tapes, toroids, rods, or thin film.

magnetic core storage: a magnetic storage in which data are stored by the selective polarization of magnetic cores.

magnetic delay line: a delay line whose operation is based on the time of propagation of magnetic waves.

magnetic disk storage: a magnetic storage in which data are stored by

112

magnetic recording on the flat surface of one or more disks that rotate in use.

magnetic domain memory: a magnetized spot representing data in bubble memory.

magnetic drum storage: a magnetic storage in which data are stored by magnetic recording on the curved surface of a cylinder that rotates in use.

magnetic head: an electromagnet that can perform one or more functions of reading, writing, and erasing data on a magnetic data medium. synonymous with *read/write head*.

magnetic ink: an ink that contains particles of a magnetic substance whose presence can be detected by magnetic sensors.

magnetic ink character recognition (MICR): recognition of characters printed with ink that contains particles of a magnetic material. cf. *optical character recognition*.

magnetic tape (MT)

(1) a tape of magnetic material used as the constituent in some forms of magnetic cores.

(2) a tape with a magnetizable surface layer on which data can be stored by magnetic recording.

magnetic thin film: a layer of magnetic material, usually less than one micron thick, often used for logic elements or storage elements.

main control unit: in a computer with more than one instruction control unit, that instruction control unit to which, for a given interval of time, the other instruction control unit may be designated as the main control unit by hardware or by hardware and software. A main control unit may be a subordinate unit at another time.

main frame

(1) *computers*: synonymous with *central processing unit*.

(2) *robotics*: the mechanical arm mechanism that consists of a series (usually three) of links and joints.

main memory (MM): usually the fastest storage device of a computer and the one from which instructions are executed. cf. *auxiliary memory*.

main storage (MS)

(1) program-addressable storage from which instructions and other data can be loaded directly into registers for subsequent execution or processing.

(2) a storage device whose storage cells can be addressed by a com-

puter program and from which instructions and data can be loaded directly into registers from which the instructions can be executed or from which the data can be operated on.

maintenance: the seventh and last phase in knowledge engineering; an ongoing phase that involves arranging to have the system revised and updated as needed. For other phases see *knowledge engineering.*

majority: a logic operator having the property that if *P* is a statement, *Q* is a statement, and *R* is a statement, . . . then the majority of *P, Q,* and *R,* . . . is true if more than half the statements are true, false if half or less are true.

major motion axes: the number of independent directions in which the arm can move the attached wrist and end effector relative to a point of origin of the manipulator such as the base. The number of robot arm axes required to reach world coordinate points is dependent on the design of the robot arm configuration. see also *world coordinate points.*

manipulation: the process of controlling and monitoring data table bits or words by means of the user's program, in order to vary application functions. The movement or reorientation of objects such as parts or tools.

manipulator: an end effector for grasping or picking up objects.

manipulator-oriented language: a programming language that describes precisely where a robot's arm and gripper should go and when. cf. *task-oriented language.*

manipulator-type robot: a means of categorizing a robot by the manipulative tasks that it can perform.

mantissa (M): the positive fractional part of the representation of a logarithm. In the expression, log 643 = 2.808; .808 is the mantissa and 2 is the characteristic. synonymous with *fixed-point part.*

manual programming: teaching a robot by physically presetting the cams on a rotating stepping drum, setting limit switches on the axes, arranging wires, or fitting air tubes.

map: to establish a set of values having a defined correspondence with the quantities or values of another set. synonymous with *map over.* see also *Karnaugh map.*

map over: synonymous with *map.*

MARGIE: an experimental language-understanding and paraphrase-generating system to demonstrate that language can be understood without attention to details of syntax.

mark: a symbol or symbols that indicate the beginning or the end of a field, word, item of data, or set of data such as a file, record, or block.

Markov chain: a probabilistic model of events in which the probability of an event is dependent only on the event that precedes it.

mark sensing: automatic sensing of conductive marks, usually recorded manually on a nonconductive data carrier. synonymous with *optical mark recognition*.

mask (MK)

(1) a pattern of characters that is used to control the retention or elimination of portions of another pattern of characters.

(2) to use a pattern of characters to control the retention or elimination of portions of another pattern of characters.

mass production: the large scale production of parts in a continuous process uninterrupted by the production of other parts.

mass storage (MS): storage having a very large capacity. synonymous with *bulk storage*.

master/slave manipulator: a teleoperator having geometrically isomorphic arms. The master is positioned by a human; the mechanical slave arm duplicates the human's movements.

match: in a production system, compares a set of patterns from the left-hand sides of rules against the data in data memory to determine all ways in which the rules can be satisfied with consistent bindings.

match cycle: the stage of processing occurring in the Rete match algorithm whenever there is a change to working memory; results in an updating of the Rete network and the conflict set.

material-handling robot: a robot programmed or designed for grasping, transporting, and positioning materials during manufacture. cf. *material-processing robot*.

material-processing robot: a robot programmed or designed to cut, form, heat-treat, finish, or process materials during manufacture. cf. *material-handling robot*.

mathematical induction: a method of providing a statement concerning terms based on natural numbers not less than N by showing that the statement is valid for the term based on N and that, if it is valid for an arbitrary value of n that is greater than N, it is also valid for the term based on $(n + 1)$.

mathematical model: a mathematical representation of a process, device, or concept.

115

matrix

(1)   in mathematics, a rectangular array of elements, arranged in rows and columns, that may be manipulated according to the rules of matrix algebra.

(2)   in computers, a logic network in the form of an array in input leads and output leads, with logic elements connected at some of their intersections.

(3)   by extension, an array of any number of dimensions.

matrix printer: a printer in which each character is represented by a pattern of dots; for example, a stylus printer or wire printer. synonymous with *dot printer*.

maximum speed: the greatest rate at which an operation can be accomplished according to a criterion of satisfaction; the greatest velocity of movement of a tool or end effector that can be achieved in producing a satisfactory result.

MBPS: see *mega*.

M-byte: see *megabyte*.

MC: see *magnetic card*.

Meaning-Representation Language: see *MRL*.

means–ends analysis: a problem-solving technique which, at every step, searches for operators that maximally lower the difference between the existing state and a known goal state.

mean time between failures (MTBF):   for a stated period in the life of a function unit, the mean value of the lengths of time between consecutive failures under stated conditions.

mean time to repair (MTTR):   the average time required for corrective maintenance.

medium technology robot: an easily transported robot with a basic mechanical and electrical control package and rather simple and rapid programming.

mega (M) (MBPS):   ten to the sixth power; 1,000,000 in decimal notation. When referring to storage capacity, two to the twentieth power; 1,048,576 in decimal notation.

megabyte (M-byte):   the number of bytes given by 2 raised to the 20th power. One M-byte is 1,048,576 bytes, or 1.048576 million bytes. The memory of most artificial intelligence systems reaches the megabyte level.

megassembly systems: multistation, multiproduct assembly systems containing at least 10 robots.

MEM: see *memory*.

member: synonymous with *element*.

memory (M) (MEM)

(1) in computers, the high speed, large capacity storage of a digital computer.

(2) in robotics, a unit into which a piece of data is entered, in which it is held, and from which it is retrieved at a later time. The robot memory is part of the controller, storing commands that have been programmed in and through the controller and telling the robot what to do and when to do it.

memory addressing: the storage locations as identified by their addresses.

memory dump: a listing of the contents of a storage device, or selected parts of it.

mental models (of human experts): symbolic networks and patterns of relationships that experts use when trying to comprehend a problem; often take the form of simplified analogies or metaphors which experts use when first examining a problem.

menu: a display of a list of available machine functions for selection by the operator.

merge

(1) to combine the items of two or more sets that are in the same given order, into one set in that order.

(2) the automatic recording, printing, or sending onto one element of recording medium of selected recorded text, in correct order, from at least two other elements of recording media.

merger sort: a sort program in which the items in a set are divided into subsets, the items in each subset are sorted, and the resulting sorted items are merged.

meta-: a prefix indicating that a term is being used to refer to itself. Thus a metarule is a rule about other rules.

metacognition: people with expertise, the knowing about complex things without being totally aware of how or why they know something.

META-DENDRAL: a learning system purporting to generate rules for DENDRAL automatically. see also *DENDRAL*.

metaknowledge: in an expert system, knowledge about how the system functions or reasons such as knowledge about the use and control of domain knowledge; knowledge about knowledge. synonymous with *metalevel knowledge.*

metalanguage: a language used to specify itself, or other languages.

metalevel knowledge: see *metaknowledge.*

Metal-Oxide Semiconductor: see *MOS.*

metarule: a rule describing how other rules should be used or modified.

Methodology for Unmanned Manufacturing (MUM): a Japanese program established to develop an unmanned factory depending heavily on robots.

MICR: see *magnetic ink character recognition.*

microcomputer: a computer system whose processing unit is a microprocessor. A basic microcomputer includes a microprocessor, storage, and an input/output facility, which may or may not be on one chip. see also *microprocessor.*

microprocessor (MP): an integrated circuit that accepts coded instructions for execution; the instructions may be entered, integrated, or stored internally. see also *microcomputer.*

mid-run explanation: the ability of a computer program to cease upon request and explain where it currently is, what it is doing, and what it will seek to accomplish next. Expert systems tend to have features that facilitate mid-run explanation while conventional programs do not.

MK: see *mask.*

ML: see *machine language.*

MM: see *main memory.*

MN: see *mnemonic.*

mnemonic (MN)

(1) a symbol chosen to assist the human memory; for example, an abbreviation such as "mpy" for "multiply."

(2) assisting or designed to assist memory.

mnemonic code: assembly language programming using words that sound similar to what they mean.

mobile robot: any robot mounted on a movable base.

mobility system: the means by which the robot moves around.

model-directed: synonymous with *backward chaining.*

modem (M)

(1) modulator-demodulator. A device that modulates and demodulates

signals transmitted over data communication facilities. see also *data set*.

(2)   a functional unit that modulates and demodulates signals. One of the functions of a modem is to enable digital data to be transmitted over analog transmission facilities.

modifier: a word or quantity used to change an instruction, causing the execution of an instruction different from the original one. The result is, the same instruction, successively changed by a modifier, can be used repeatedly to carry out a different operation each time it is used.

modular

(1)   in computers, a degree of standardization of system components to allow for combinations and a large variety of compatible units.

(2)   in robotics, a robot constructed from a number of interchangeable subunits, each of which can be one of a range of sizes or have one of several possible motion styles and number of axes.

modulator-demodulator: see *modem*.

modulo-N check: synonymous with *residue check*.

modulo-N counter: a counter in which the number represented reverts to zero in the sequence of counting after reaching a maximum value of $N-1$.

modus ponens: a basic rule of logic that asserts that if we know that A implies B and we know for a fact that A is true, we can assume B.

MON: see *monitor*.

monadic operation: an operation with one and only one operand.

monitor (MON) (MTR)

(1)   a device that observes and verifies the operations of a data processing system, and indicates any significant departure from the norm.

(2)   software or hardware that observes, supervises, controls, or verifies the operations of a system.

monotonic reasoning: a reasoning system based on the assumption that once a fact is determined, it cannot be altered during the course of the reasoning process; thus, once the user has answered a question, the system assumes that the answer will remain the same throughout the session. MYCIN is a monotonic system.

Monte Carlo method: a method of obtaining an approximate solution to a numerical problem by the use of random numbers; for example, the random walk method or a procedure using a random number sequence to calculate an integral.

MOS: Metal-Oxide Semiconductor. A technology that helped make possible new types of complex chips, such as the microprocessor used in personal computers and high-capacity memories. see also *CMOS*.

MP

(1) see *microprocessor*.

(2) see *multiprocessor*.

MPLX: see *multiplexer*.

MPLXR: see *multiplexer*.

MPS: see *multiprocessing system*.

MPX: see *multiplexer*.

MRL: Meaning-Representation Language. An extended first order predicate calculus language with classes; used as a formal language for representing objects and their interrelations.

MS

(1) see *main storage*.

(2) see *mass storage*.

MT: see *magnetic tape*.

MTBF: see *mean time between failures*.

MTR: see *monitor*.

MTTR: see *mean time to repair*.

MUL: see *multiplexer*.

multimode: a descriptor of programs that functions in different modes.

multipass sort: a sort program that is designed to sort more items than can be in main storage at one time.

multiple lines of reasoning: a problem-solving method where a limited number of possibly independent approaches to solving a problem are developed in parallel.

multiple-precision: pertaining to the use of two or more computer words to represent a number in order to enhance precision.

multiplex

(1) to interleave or simultaneously transmit two or more messages on a single channel.

(2) the process or equipment for combining a number of individual channels into a common spectrum or a common bit stream for transmission.

multiplexer (MPLX) (MPLXR) (MPX) (MUL) (MUX): a device capable of interleaving the events of two or more activities, or of distributing the events of an interleaved sequence to the respective activities.

120

multiprocessing system (MPS): a computing system employing two or more interconnected processing units to execute programs simultaneously.

multiprocessor (MP)
(1) a computer employing two or more processing units under integrated control.
(2) a system consisting of two or more processing units. Arithmetic logic units or processors that can communicate without manual intervention.

multiprocessor control: a procedure where two or more control subtracks of the same overall control system can be accomplished simultaneously by more than one CPU.

multiprogramming
(1) pertaining to the concurrent execution of two or more computer programs by a computer. synonymous with *concurrent execution.*
(2) a mode of operation that provides for the interleaved execution of two or more computer programs by a single processor.

multitasking: a hardware installation and an operating system configuration that lets a user perform two or more tasks simultaneously.

multiuser: a hardware installation and operating system configuration that lets more than one person use the resources of the system at the same apparent time.

multivalued attribute: an attribute having more than one value; for example, if a system seeks values for the attribute car, and if car is multivalued, then two or more cars may be identified.

MUM: see *Methodology for Unmanned Manufacturing.*

MUX: see *multiplexer.*

MYCIN: an expert system developed at Stanford University in the mid-1970s; a research system originally designed to aid physicians in the diagnosis and treatment of meningitis and bacteremia infections. MYCIN is often referred to as the first expert system combining all of the major features with the clear separation of the knowledge base and the inference engine. This separation, in turn, led to the subsequent development of the first expert system building tool, EMYCIN.

N

N: see *node.*

NAK: see *negative acknowledge character.*

NAND: a logic operation having the property that if *P* is a statement, *Q* is a statement, *R* is a statement, . . . then the NAND of *P, Q, R,* . . . *T* is true if at least one statement is false, false if all statements are true. synonymous with *nonconjunction; NOT-AND; Sheffer stroke.*

NAND element: a logic element that performs the boolean operation of nonconjunction. synonymous with *NAND gate.*

NAND gate: synonymous with *NAND element.*

nanosecond (NS) (NSEC): one-thousand-millionth of a second; one billionth of a second.

narrow system building tools: see *large, narrow system building tools.*

n-ary

(1) pertaining to a selection, choice or condition that has *n* possible different values or states.

(2) pertaining to a fixed-radix numeration system having a radix of *n.*

natural language

(1) *general:* a language whose rules are based on current usage without being specifically prescribed.

(2) *artificial intelligence:* a branch of artificial intelligence research that studies methods permitting computer systems to accept inputs and produce outputs in a conventional language like English.

natural language understanding and translation: in artificial intelligence where experts develop software permitting a user to interact with a computer system via spoken or written statements.

natural number: one of the numbers 0, 1, 2, ... synonymous with *nonnegative number.*

n-bit byte: a byte composed of *n* binary elements.

NC: see *numerical control.*

n-**core-per-bit storage:** a storage device in which each storage cell uses *n* magnetic cores per binary character.

near miss: a counterexample of a concept similar to positive examples of this concept; useful in isolating significant features in learning from examples.

near-miss analysis: exploiting near misses to bound the scope of generalization in learning from examples. see *generalization; near miss.*

negation: the monadic boolean operation the result of which has the boolean value opposite to that of the operand. synonymous with *NOT operation.*

negative acknowledge character (NAK): in binary synchronous communication, a line control character sent by a receiving terminal to indicate that an error was encountered in the previous transmission, and that the receiving terminal is ready to accept another transmission.

negative example: in learning from examples, a counterexample of a concept bound by the scope of generalization. see *generalization; learning from examples.*

neper: a unit for measuring power. The number of nepers is the logarithm (base *e*) of the ratio of the measured power levels.

nest

(1) to incorporate a structure or structures of some kind into a structure of the same kind; for example, to nest one loop (the nested loop) within another loop (the nesting loop); to nest one subroutine (the nested subroutine) within another subroutine (the nesting subroutine).

(2) to embed subroutines or data in other subroutines or data at a different hierarchical level, such that the different levels of routines or data can be executed or accessed recursively.

net load capacity: the added weight or mass of a material that is handled by a machine or process without failure, over and above that needed for a container, pallet, or other device that necessarily accompanies the material.

network: computers and communication links that permit computers to communicate with each other and to share programs, facilities, and data and knowledge bases. A network can be local (one room, one office, one institution), national, or even international.

network analog: the expression and solution of mathematical relationships between variables, using a circuit or circuits to represent these variables.

network node: synonymous with *node.*

neural-net systems: synonymous with *neural-network computers.*

neural-network computers: computers with circuits patterned after the complex interconnections among nerve cells in the brain. Provides speeds unmatched by traditional computers for placing or removing data in storage; for sorting through large data bases to find close matches; and independently formulates methods of processing data. synonymous with *neural-net systems.*

new-line character (NL): a format effector that causes the print or display position to move to the first position on the next line.

nines complement: the diminished radix complement in the decimal numeration system. synonymous with *complement-on-nine.*

NL: see *new-line character.*

***n*-level address:** an indirect address that specifies *n* levels of addressing.

NOAH: an expert system for planning robotics projects.

node (N)

(1) the representation of a state or an event by means of a point on a diagram.

(2) in a tree structure, a point at which subordinate items of data originate.

(3) in a data network, a point at which one or more functional units interconnect data transmission lines.

(4) synonymous with *network node.*

noise

(1) random variations of one or more characteristics of any entity such as voltage, current, or data.

(2) a random signal of known statistical properties of amplitude, distribution, and spectral density.

(3) loosely, any disturbance tending to interfere with the normal operation of a device or system.

nonconjunction: synonymous with *NAND.*

noncontact sensors: see *photoelectric proximity sensors; proximity sensors.*

nondisjunction: synonymous with *NOR.*

nonequivalence operation: the dyadic boolean operation the result of which has the boolean value 1 if and only if the operand has different boolean values.

125

nonidentity operation: the boolean operation the result of which has the boolean value 1 if and only if all the operands do not have the same boolean value. A nonidentity operation on two operands is a nonequivalence operation. cf. *identity operation.*

nonlinear optimization: synonymous with *nonlinear programming.*

nonlinear programming: in operations research, a procedure for locating the maximum or minimum (or both) of a function of variables that is subject to constraints, as nonlinear. synonymous with *nonlinear optimization.* cf. *convex programming; dynamic programming; linear programming.*

nonmonotonic reasoning: reasoning that can be revised if some value changes during a session; can deal with problems that involve rapid changes in values in short periods of time.

nonnegative number: synonymous with *natural number.*

non-return-to-change recording: a method of recording in which ones are represented by a specified condition of magnetization and zeros are represented by a different condition.

non-return-to-reference recording: the magnetic recording of binary digits such that the patterns of magnetization used to represent zeros and ones occupy the whole storage cell, with no part of the cell magnetized to the reference condition. synonymous with *non-return-to-zero recording.*

non-return-to-zero recording: synonymous with *non-return-to-reference recording.*

nonservo robot: a high speed robot, having a relatively small size manipulator and full flow of air or oil through control valves, with limited flexibility of program capacity and positioning capability.

nontransparent mode: a mode of binary synchronous transmission in which all control characters are treated as control characters (i.e., not treated as text).

no-op: see *no-operation instruction.*

no-operation instruction (no-op): an instruction whose execution causes a computer to do nothing other than to proceed to the next instruction to be executed. synonymous with *do-nothing operation.*

NOR: a logic operator having the property that if P is a statement, Q is a statement, R is a statement, . . . then the NOR of $P, Q, R, . . .$ is true if all statements are false, false if at least one statement is true. P NOR Q is often represented by a combination of OR and NOT symbols such as (*PVQ*). *N* NOR *Q* is called neither *P* NOR *Q*. synonymous with *nondisjunction; NOT-OR.*

NOT: a logic operator having the property that if *P* is a statement, then the NOT of *P* is true if *P* is false, false if *P* is true.

NOT-AND: synonymous with *NAND.*

notation: a set of symbols and the rules for their use, for the representation of data.

NOT element: a logic element that performs the boolean operation of negation. synonymous with *NOT gate.*

NOT gate: synonymous with *NOT element.*

NOT-IF-THEN operation: synonymous with *exclusion.*

NOT operation: synonymous with *negation.*

NOT-OR: synonymous with *NOR.*

noughts complement: synonymous with *radix complement.*

NS: see *nanosecond.*

NSEC: see *nanosecond.*

NUL: see *null character.*

null: empty; having no meaning; not usable.

null character (NUL): a control character that is used to accomplish media-fill or time-fill, and which may be inserted into or removed from a sequence of characters without affecting the meaning of the sequence; however, the control of equipment or the format may be affected by this character.

numerical analysis: the study of methods of obtaining useful quantitative solutions to problems that have been expressed mathematically, including the study of the errors and bounds on errors in obtaining such solutions.

numerical control (NC): the automatic control of a process performed by a device that makes use of numeric data, usually introduced while the operation is in progress.

numeric character: synonymous with *digit.*

numeric character set: a character set that contains digits and may contain control characters, special characters, and the space character, but not letters. cf. *numeric character subset.*

numeric character subset: a character subset that contains digits and may contain control characters, special characters, and the space character, but not letters. cf. *numeric character set.*

numeric code: a code according to which data are represented by a numeric character set.

numeric word: a word consisting of digits and possibly the space character and special characters; for example, in the Universal Decimal Classification system, the numeric word 61 (03) = 20 is used as an identifier for any medical encyclopedia in English.

O

O
    (1) see *operand.*
    (2) see *operation.*
    (3) see *operator.*

O-A-V triplets: see *object-attribute-value triplets.*

object: synonymous with *frame.*

object-attribute-value triplets: synonymous with *context-parameter-value triplets.*

object code: output from a compiler or assembler that is itself an executable machine code, or is suitable for processing to produce executable machine code(s).

objective function: the independent variable function whose maximum or minimum is sought in an optimization problem.

object language: synonymous with *target language.*

object-oriented language: in robotics, synonymous with *task-oriented language.*

object-oriented techniques: programming procedures based on the use of items called objects that communicate with one another via messages in the form of global broadcasts.

object program: synonymous with *target program.*

object tree: synonymous with *context tree.*

OCR: see *optical character recognition.*

OCT: see *octal.*

octal (OCT): pertaining to a fixed-radix numeration system having a radix of eight.

octopod: an eight-legged walking robot. cf. *biped.*

odd-even check: synonymous with *parity check.*

ODR: see *optical data recognition.*

OF: see *overflow.*

off-line: pertaining to the operation of a function unit without the continual control of a computer.

off-line storage: storage that is not under the control of the processing unit.

offset branching: a method used by a robot system to create a branch that can be used at a number of points in the robot cycle, and that can affect its sequence relative to the physical location of the robot arm when the branch is requested. The entire branch is offset about the robot's position and/or the wrist orientation.

OFL: see *overflow.*

OL: see *on-line.*

OMR: see *optical mark recognition; mark sensing.*

one-dimensional language: a language whose expressions are customarily represented as strings of characters; for example, FORTRAN.

one-input node: a node in the Rete match algorithm network associated with a test of a single attribute of a condition element; passes a token if and only if the attribute test has been satisfied.

one-plus-one address instruction: an instruction that contains two address parts, the plus-one address being that part of the instruction that is to be executed next unless otherwise specified.

ones complement: the diminished radix complement in the pure binary numeration system. synonymous with *complement-on-one.*

on-line (OL)
(1)   pertaining to a user's ability to interact with a computer.
(2)   pertaining to a user's access to a computer via a terminal.
(3)   pertaining to the operation of a functional unit that is under the continual control of a computer.

on-line storage: storage that is under the control of the processing unit.

on-line system: a system in which the input data enter the computer directly from the point of origin or in which output data are transmitted directly to where they are used.

OP
(1)   see *operand.*
(2)   see *operation.*
(3)   see *operator.*

OPD: see *operand.*

open code: in assembler programming, that portion of a source module that lies outside of and after any source macrodefinitions that may be specified.

open-loop control: where the central processing unit does not directly control a process or procedure but instead displays or prints information for the operator to assist in an action-oriented decision.

open-loop robot: a robot that incorporates no feedback, that is, no means of comparing actual output to commanded input of position or rate.

open subroutine: a subroutine of which a replica must be inserted at each place in a computer program where the subroutine is used. synonymous with *direct insert subroutine.* cf. *closed subroutine.*

operand (O) (OP) (OPD)

(1)   an entity to which an operation is applied.

(2)   that which is operated on. An operand is usually identified by an address part of an instruction.

(3)   information entered with a command name to define the data on which a command processor operates and to control the execution of the command processor.

operating system (OS): software that controls the execution of a computer program, and that may provide scheduling, debugging, input/output control, accounting, compilation, storage assignment, data management, and related services.

operating time: that part of available time during which the hardware is operating and is assumed to be yielding correct results. It includes program development time, production time, makeup time, and miscellaneous time.

operation (O) (OP)

(1)   a well-defined action that, when applied to any permissible combination of known entities, produces a new entity.

(2)   a defined action, namely, the act of obtaining a result from one or more operands in accordance with a rule that completely specifies the result for any permissible combination of operands.

(3)   a program set undertaken or executed by a computer; for example, addition, multiplication, extraction, comparison, shift, transfer. The operation is usually specified by the operator part of an instruction.

(4)   the event or specific action performed by a logic element.

operational amplifier: a high-gain amplifier that is the basic component

131

of analog computing elements; this amplifier performs specified computing operations or provides specified transfer functions.

operationalization: synonymous with *knowledge compilation.*

operation table: a table that defines an operation by listing all permissible combinations of values of the operands and indicating the result for each of these combinations. see *boolean operation table.*

operator (O) (OP) (OPR)

(1) a symbol that represents the action to be performed in a mathematical operation.

(2) in the description of a process, that which indicates the action to be performed on operands.

(3) a person who operates a machine.

OPR: see *operator.*

OPS: a combination language, operating system, and software package suited to the development of expert systems. Developed at Carnegie-Mellon University specifically for developing expert systems and used for developing R1, it is one of the first successful expert systems.

OPS5: see *production system.* see also *OPS.*

OPS83: a second-generation version of OPS5 that incorporates an imperative sublanguage and new compiler technology that makes it run substantially faster than the LISP-based version. cf. *OPS5.*

optical character recognition (OCR)

(1) the machine identification of printed characters through use of light-sensitive devices.

(2) character recognition that uses optical means to identify graphic characters. cf. *magnetic ink character recognition.*

optical data recognition (ODR): any form of optical recognition of data, including optical mark readers, document readers, and page readers.

optical document reader: an optical reading unit that scans or reads only a small portion of an input document and that is limited to a few type styles or fonts.

optical mark recognition (OMR): synonymous with *mark sensing.*

optical page reader: an optical reading unit that scans an entire page or document and that may have the capability of reading many type styles.

optical scanner

(1) a scanner that uses light for examining patterns.

(2) a device that scans optically and usually generates an analog or digital signal.

optic sensor: a device or system that converts light into an electrical signal.

optimal control: a control method whereby the system response to a commanded input is optimal according to a specified objective function or criterion of performance, given the dynamics of the process to be controlled and the constraints on measuring.

optimization: see *satisfice.*

optional-halt instruction: synonymous with *optional-pause instruction.*

optional-pause instruction: an instruction that allows manual suspension of the execution of a computer program. synonymous with *optional-halt instruction; optional-stop instruction.* see also *pause instruction.*

optional-stop instruction: synonymous with *optional-pause instruction.*

OR: a logic operator having the property that if P is a statement, Q is a statement, R is a statement, . . . then the OR of $P, Q, R,$ . . . is true if at least one statement is true, false if all statements are false. P OR Q is often represented by $P + Q$, PVQ. synonymous with *boolean ADD.*

ordering: a conflict resolution strategy in which the dominance of one instantiation over another is determined by a static ordering imposed on the rules.

or node: see *and/or tree.*

OR operation: synonymous with *disjunction.*

OS: see *operating system.*

output contacts: switch contacts operated by a robot that provide the robot with control such as turning on or off motors, heaters, grippers, welding equipment, and so on. Controlling output contacts becomes part of the robot routine. Whenever that routine is replayed, that contact is closed (opened) at the same point at which it was taught.

OV: see *overflow.*

overflow (OF) (OFL) (OV) (OVF)

(1) that portion of a word expressing the result of an operation by which its word length exceeds the storage capacity of the intended storage device. synonymous with *arithmetic overflow.*

(2) that portion of the result of an operation that exceeds the capacity of the intended unit of storage.

(3) in a register, loss of one or more of the leftmost whole-number digits because the result of an operation exceeded 10 digits.

overhead operation: synonymous with *housekeeping operation.*

133

overshoot

(1)   when a control device carries the controlled variable or output past a final or desired value.

(2)   the amount that an output pulse momentarily exceeds its stabilized value.

OVF: see *overflow.*

P

P
  (1) see *parallel*.
  (2) see *processor*.
  (3) see *program*.

package: in LISP, a data structure determining the mapping from print names (strings) to LISP symbols; a means of ensuring that entities used by LISP are uniquely named, thereby avoiding name collisions. see also *package cell*.

package cell: in a symbol's data structure, contains the entry that points to the package that owns the symbols.

packed decimal: the representation of decimal value by two adjacent digits in a byte; for example, in packed decimal, the decimal value 23 is represented by 00100011. cf. *unpacked decimal*.

packed density: the number of storage cells per unit length, unit area, or unit volume; for example, the number of bits per inch stored on a magnetic tape track or magnetic drum track.

packet: a sequence of binary digits including data and call control signals that is switched as a composite whole. The data, call control signals, and, possibly, error control information are arranged in a specific format.

pad
  (1) to fill a block with dummy data, usually zeros or blanks.
  (2) a device which introduces transmission loss into a circuit. It may be inserted to introduce loss or match impedances.

page (PG)
  (1) a block of instructions and/or data that can be located in main storage or in auxiliary storage. Segmentation and loading of these blocks is automatically controlled by a computer.
  (2) in a virtual storage system, a fixed-length block that has a virtual

address and that can be transferred between real storage and auxiliary storage.

(3) to transfer instructions, data, or both between real storage and external page storage.

palletizing: placing parts in position.

paradigm: see *consultation paradigm.*

paragraph: a set of one or more COBOL sentences, making up a logical processing entity, and preceded by a paragraph name or a paragraph header.

parallel (P)

(1) pertaining to the concurrent or simultaneous operation of two or more devices or to the concurrent performance of two or more activities in a single device.

(2) pertaining to the concurrent or simultaneous occurrence of two or more related activities in multiple devices or channels.

(3) pertaining to the simultaneity of two or more processes.

(4) pertaining to the simultaneous processing of the individual parts of a whole such as the bits of a character and the characters of a word, using separate facilities for the various parts. cf. *serial.*

parallel adder: a digital adder in which addition is performed concurrently on digits in all the digit places of the operands.

parallel communications: a digital communication method for transmitting several bits of a message at a time (usually 8 to 17). Used only over distances of a few feet, with electrical cables as the transmission medium.

parallel computer: a computer having multiple arithmetic or logic units that are used to accomplish parallel operations or parallel processing.

parallel processing (PP): the concurrent or simultaneous execution of two or more processes in a single unit.

parameter (PARM)

(1) a variable that is given a constant value for a specified application and that may denote the application.

(2) a variable that is given a constant value for a specific document processing program instruction; for example, left margin 10.

(3) a name in a procedure that is used to refer to an argument passed to that procedure.

parameter word: a word that directly or indirectly provides or designates one or more parameters.

136

parity bit: a binary digit appended to a group of binary digits to make the sum of all the digits either always odd (odd parity) or always even (even parity).

parity check: a check to test whether the number of ones (or zeros) in an array of binary digits is odd or even. synonymous with *odd-even check*.

PARM: see *parameter*.

part classification: a coding method, typically involving four or more digits, that specifies a discrete product as belonging to a part family. see *part family*.

part family: a set of discrete products that is produced by the same sequence of machining operations; primarily associated with group technology. see also *part classification*.

partial bindings: the set of working memory elements and bindings that constitutes a consistent binding for a prefix sequence of condition elements of a rule.

partially learned concept: in concept learning, an underdetermined concept; that is, a concept whose precise description cannot be inferred based on a learner's current data, knowledge, and assumptions. see also *incremental learning; version space*.

partial matching: a method for comparing structural descriptions by identifying their corresponding components.

part orientation: the angular displacement of a product being manufactured relative to a coordinate system referenced to a production machine.

passive accommodation: compliant behavior of a robot's end point in response to forces exerted on it. No sensors, controls, or actuator are involved. The remote center compliance provides this in a coordinate system located at the tip of a gripped part.

passive mode: in computer graphics, a mode of operation of a display device that does not allow an on-line user to alter or interact with a display image.

patch
  (1)   a temporary electrical connection.
  (2)   to make an improvised modification.
  (3)   to modify a routine in a rough or expedient way.

path constraint: in problem solving, a predicate on partial solution sequences; a type of constraint. see also *predicate*.

path planning approach: see *continuous-path control.*

pattern: an abstract description of a datum that places certain constraints on the value(s) it may assume, but need not specify it in complete detail.

pattern-directed: driven by configurations of data, as in a production system.

pattern matching: a process where agreement is found between a given situation and a set of criteria characterizing a standard situation. The agreement may only be partial.

pattern recognition

(1) the identification of shapes, forms, or configurations by automatic means.

(2) the classification or description of pictures or other data structures into a set of categories or classes; a subset of the subject artificial intelligence.

pause instruction: an instruction that specifies the suspension of the execution of a computer program. A pause instruction is usually not an exit. synonymous with *halt instruction.* see *optional-pause instruction.*

payload: the maximum weight or mass of a material that can be handled satisfactorily by a machine or process in normal and continuous operation.

pedestal sensor: see *force sensor.*

pendant: a teaching pendant attached to the robot for control purposes. see also *teaching pendant.*

perception: the robot's ability to sense its environment by sight, touch, or some other means and to understand it in terms of a task; for example, the ability to recognize an obstruction or find a designated object in an arbitrary location.

PERF: see *performance.*

perforated tape: synonymous with *punched tape.*

performance (PERF): together with a facility, one of the two major factors on which the total productivity of a system depends. Performance is largely determined by a combination of three other factors: throughput, response time, and availability.

performance aids: synonymous with *job aids.*

peripheral control unit: synonymous with *input/output controller.*

peripheral equipment: in a data processing system, any equipment, distinct from the central processing unit, that may provide the system outside communication or additional facilities.

permanent storage: synonymous with *read-only storage.*

permutation: an ordered arrangement of a given number of different elements selected from a set.

PG: see *page.*

PGM: see *program.*

phase modulation (PM)

(1) modulation in which the phase angle of a carrier is the characteristic varied.

(2) angle modulation in which the phase angle of a sinusoidal carrier is caused to vary from a reference carrier phase angle by an amount proportional to the instantaneous amplitude of the modulating signal.

photoelectric proximity (noncontact) sensors: a version of the photoelectric tube and light source; sensors appear to be well adapted for controlling the motion of a manipulator. They consist of a solid-state light-emitting diode (LED) which acts as a transmitter of infrared light, and a solid-state light diode, which acts as a receiver, both mounted in a small package. Such sensors are sensitive to objects located from a fraction of an inch to several feet in front of the sensor.

photo-isolator: a solid-state device that allows complete electrical isolation between the field wiring and the controller.

photoresistor: a unit for measuring light whose resistance changes as a function of incident light.

pick-and-place robot: an elementary robot possessing only two or three degrees of freedom; able to shift goods from one place to another with no trajectory control. synonymous with *bang-bang robot.*

picosecond (PS): one trillionth of a second; one thousandth of a nanosecond.

PID: see *proportional-integral-derivative control.*

pin board: a perforated board into which pins are manually inserted to control the operation of equipment. synonymous with *plugboard.*

pitch: see *wrist movement.*

pixel: a picture element; the small region of a scene within which variations of brightness are ignored.

PLANNER: an extinct experimental programming language similar to PROLOG. see *PROLOG.*

plasma panel: a part of a display device that consists of a grid of electrodes in a flat, gas-filled panel in which the energizing of selected electrodes causes the gas to be ionized and light to be emitted at that point. synonymous with *gas panel.*

plausible inference: a derivation of likely conclusions from incomplete, imperfect, or indirectly relevant premises.

playback accuracy

(1) the difference between a position command recorded in an automatic control system and that actually produced at a later time when the recorded position is used for executing control.

(2) the difference between actual position response of an automatic control system during a programming or teaching run and that corresponding response in a subsequent run.

PLC: see *programmable logic controller.*

PL/1: Programming Language 1. A programming language designed for numeric scientific computations, business data processing, systems programming, and other applications. PL/1 is capable of handling a large variety of data structures and easily allows variation of precision in numeric computation.

plotter: an output unit that presents data in the form of a two-dimensional graphic representation.

plugboard: synonymous with *pin board.*

plug-in programming: see *programming.*

PM: see *phase modulation.*

pneumatic: control by use of air pressure.

pointer: in software, a number indicating the location of an object in memory.

point-to-point control: a control method wherein the inputs or commands specify only a limited number of points along a desired path of motion. The control system determines the intervening path segments.

point-to-point robot: a robot in which each axis is shifted separately until the combination of axis positions yields the preferred position of the robot end effector, which is then programmed into memory, thus storing the individual position of each axis.

polar coordinate system: a coordinate system, two of whose dimensions are angles, the third being a linear distance from the point of origin. These three coordinates specify a point on a sphere.

Polish notation: synonymous with *prefix notation.*

POLITICS: an experimental narrative-understanding natural language system that is a successor to MARGIE and the predecessor of BORIS.

polling

(1) interrogation of devices for purposes such as avoiding contention, determining operational status, or determining readiness to send or receive data.

(2) the process whereby stations are invited, one at a time, to transmit.

polyphase sort: an unbalanced merge sort in which the distribution of sort subsets is based on a Fibonacci series.

POP: slang; to get information from the stack.

port: an access point for data entry or exit.

portable standard LISP (PSL): a dialect of LISP.

POS: see *position.*

position (POS)

(1) a site on a punched tape or card where holes are to be punched.

(2) a place in a program, set of instructions, or context.

(3) in a string, each location occupied by a character or binary element that may be identified by a serial number.

position control: a control system in which the input (desired output) is the position of some body.

position error: in a servomechanism that controls a manipulator joint, the difference between the actual position of that joint and the commanded position.

positioning accuracy and repeatability: accuracy is the measure of a robot's ability to move to a programmed position; repeatability is its ability to do this time after time. With the pick-and-place robot, accuracy and repeatability are interchangeable. With a programmable robot, repeatability can be improved by fine-tuning the controls.

positive example: in learning from examples, a correct instance of a concept resulting in generalization.

postamble: a sequence of binary characters recorded at the end of each block on phase-encoded magnetic tape for the purpose of synchronization when reading backward.

postcondition: a proposition that is true following execution of a piece of code. Should a precondition be satisfied preceding the execution of the code, and if the code executes correctly, the postcondition will be true following execution.

postfix notation: a method of forming mathematical expressions in which each operator is preceded by its operands and indicates the operation to be performed on the operands or the intermediate results

141

that precede it. synonymous with *reverse Polish notation; suffix notation.* cf. *prefix notation.*

Post production system: a mathematical model of computation considered to be the origin of all other production systems; created by Emil Post.

potentiometer: a disk-type resistor with two fixed terminals and a third terminal connected to a variable contact arm.

power supply
(1) *computers:* a unit that converts the line voltage from a wall socket into the voltages needed by the computer elements.
(2) *robotics:* the power supply that provides energy to the manipulator's actuators. With electrically driven robots, the power supply functions basically to regulate the incoming electrical energy. Power for pneumatically actuated robots is usually supplied by a remote compressor, which also services other devices.

power tool: any powerful programming device that significantly increases programmer productivity.

PP: see *parallel processing.*

pragmatics: the relationship of characters or groups of characters to their interpretation and use.

preamble: a sequence of binary architecture recorded at the beginning of each block on a phase-encoded magnetic tape for the purpose of synchronization.

precision
(1) a measure of the ability to distinguish between nearly equal values.
(2) the degree of discrimination with which a quantity is stated; for example, a three-digit numeral discriminates among one thousand possibilities. cf. *accuracy.*

precondition: a proposition that must be satisfied preceding the execution of a piece of code. If the precondition is satisfied and the code executes correctly, a postcondition will be true following execution of the code.

predicate: a function of one or more arguments, returning a value true or false.

predicate calculus: an extension of propositional calculus. Each elementary unit in predicate calculus is called an object. Statements about objects are called predicates.

prefix notation: a method of forming mathematical expressions in which each operator precedes its operands and indicates the operation to be performed on the operands or the intermediate results that follow it. synonymous with *Lukasiewics notation; Polish notation.* cf. *infix notation; postfix notation.*

presence sensing device: a device designed, constructed and installed to create a sensing field or area around a robot that will detect an intrusion into such field or area by a person, robot, and so on.

preset: to establish an initial condition, such as the control values of a loop, or the value to which a parameter is to be bound.

presumptive instruction: an instruction that is not an effective instruction until it has been modified in a prescribed manner.

preview control: see *continuous-path control.*

primary storage unit: synonymous with *internal storage.*

print name: the literal string name of a LISP symbol.

probability: various approaches to statistical inference used for determining the likelihood of a particular relationship. Expert systems have generally avoided probability and used confidence factors instead. cf. *certainty.*

probability propagation: the adjusting of probabilities at the nodes in an inference net accounting for the effect of new information about the probability at a specific node.

problem-oriented language: a programming language that is suitable for a specific class of problems. Procedure-oriented languages such as FORTRAN, ALGOL; simulation languages such as GPSS, SIMSCRIPT; listing processing languages such as LISP, IPL-V; information retrieval languages. synonymous with *application-oriented language.*

problem reformulation: translating a problem statement into an alternative statement so that an appropriate solution method can be applied.

problem-solving method: a procedure (either an algorithm or a heuristic) for determining a solution to a problem.

problem space: a conceptual or formal area defined by all of the possible states that could occur as a result of interactions between elements and operators that are considered when a specific problem is studied.

PROC: see *processor.*

proceduralization: converting declarative knowledge into procedural form. see also *knowledge compilation.*

procedural knowledge: knowledge that is immediately executed utilizing declarative knowledge as data but that may not be examined.

procedural language: a computer language where language-level instruction mirroring, Von Neumann machine instructions, and the state of an execution are defined by a program counter.

procedural versus declarative: two complementary views of a computer program. Procedures tell a system what to do (e.g., multiple A times B and then add C). Declarations tell a system what to know (e.g., $V = IR$).

procedure

(1) a set of instruction for performing a task.

(2) a program embodying an algorithm or a heuristic.

(3) a syntactic unit of a program in a procedural language that can be parameterized so that the same segment of code can be invoked from different places in the program with different data.

(4) any representation for procedural knowledge.

procedure-oriented methods: programming strategy utilizing nested subroutines for organizing and controlling program execution.

processor (P) (PROC)

(1) in a computer, a functional unit that interprets and executes instructions.

(2) a functional unit, part of another unit such as a terminal or a processing unit, that interprets and executes instructions.

processor storage: synonymous with *internal storage.*

production: an if-then statement or rule representing knowledge in a human's long-term memory.

production memory: the set of all rules in a production system.

production node: a special node in the Rete match algorithm network that associates a rule with the set of nodes that tests whether the rule's conditions are satisfied.

production rule: used by cognitive psychologists to describe an *if-then* rule.

production system: a human or computer system having a data base of production rules and some control mechanism that chooses applicable production rules in an effort to reach some goal state. OPS5 is an expert system building tool that is a production system; it was initially developed in an effort to model supposed human mental operations.

production-system language: a computer language employing as a prominent component an architecture that is a production system.

production-system model: a style of problem solving and programming characterized by a production-system architecture.

production-system program: an application program written in a production-system language and in which a major portion of the problem is accomplished by the firing of rules.

PROG: see *program.*

program (P) (PGM) (PROG)
(1) to design, write, and test programs.
(2) a set of actions or instructions that a machine is capable of interpreting and executing.
(3) a schedule or plan that specifies actions that may or may not be taken.

program generator: synonymous with *report generator.*

program interrupt: applied to the automatic interrupting of regular program operation whenever an I/O unit becomes available.

program loop: a series of instructions that may be executed repeatedly in accordance with the logic of the program.

programmable: capable of being instructed to operate in a specified manner, or of accepting set points or other commands from a remote source.

programmable controller: a solid-state control system that has a user programmable memory for storage of instructions to implement specific functions such as I/O control logic, timing, counting, arithmetic, and data manipulation; consists of a central processor, input/output interface, memory, and programming device which typically uses relay-equivalent symbols. The programmable controller is purposely designed as an industrial control system that can perform functions equivalent to a relay panel or a wired solid-state logic control system.

programmable logic controller (PLC): a stored program unit intended to replace relay logic used in sequencing, timing, and counting of discrete events.

programmable manipulator: a unit able to manipulate objects by executing a stored program residing in its memory.

programmable read-only memory (PROM): an integrated circuit of read-only memory that can be programmed by a user; for example, following manufacture, by means of a hardware device known as a PROM programmer.

programmer's apprentice: a system for aiding programmers by maintaining track of decisions, recalling program skeletons, automatically testing revised programs, supporting natural language interaction, and translating to and from various program representations.

programming

(1) *computers:* the designing, writing, and testing of programs. synonymous with *software engineering.*

(2) *robotics:* a means to enable the robot to perform the required tasks; accomplished in the following ways: (a) *lead-through,* where the robot is placed in the teach mode of operation and points in space are recorded as the robot is led through the desired sequence, (b) *walkthrough,* where the robot is placed in the teach mode of operation and manually walked through the desired sequence of movements and operations, (c) *plug-in,* where a prerecorded program is physically transferred into the robot control, usually through the use of magnetic tape, and (d) *computer programming,* where robots are programmed through the use of computer programs written especially for the computers being used to control the robot actions.

programming environment: an environment about halfway between a language and a tool. A language permits the user complete flexibility. A tool constrains the user in many ways. A programming environment (like INTERLISP) provides a number of established routines that can facilitate the quick development of certain types of programs. cf. *development environment.*

Programming Language 1: see *PL/1.*

program unit

(1) in FORTRAN, a main program or a subprogram.

(2) a simple and flexible unit that permits programs for automatic card punching operation to be easily prepared and inserted.

PROLOG: a symbolic or artificial intelligence programming language based on predicate calculus; the most popular language for artificial intelligence research outside of North America.

PROM: see *programmable read-only memory.*

pronation: the orientation or motion toward a position with the back (or protected) side facing up or exposed.

146

proof tree: a tree data structure in which the root node represents a theorem to be proved, and the children of each node represent theorems that, when proved, suffice to prove the theorem represented by their parent. A proof tree may be an *and/or tree.* see also *and/or tree.*

properties: see *property.*

property

(1) *general:* a characteristic of an object having values called *attributes.* Components of frames and schemas, which can be of arbitrary complexity, are sometimes called *properties.*

(2) *LISP:* an entry in a property list. Collectively, describes an object, being a name, definition, or value of an object. see also *property list.*

property list: in LISP, when associated with a LISP symbol, has zero or more entries, depending on the LISP symbol and when it is used. see also *property.*

proportional control: a control technique whereby the signal that drives the actuator equals the difference between the input (desired output) and measured actual output.

proportional-integral-derivative control (PID): a control method whereby the signal that drives the actuator equals a weighted sum of the difference, time integral of the difference, and time derivative of the difference between the input (desired output) and the measured actual output.

proprioceptors: in robotics, a component that senses the posture of a mechanical manipulator, legs, or other jointed mechanism.

PROSPECTOR: an experimental expert system intended to help geologists interpret mineral data, and predict the location of mineral deposits.

prosthetic units: artificial limbs and replacements for various parts of the body.

protocol

(1) a specification for the format and relative timing of information exchanged between communicating parties.

(2) the set of rules governing the operation of functional units of a communication that must be followed if communication is to be achieved. synonymous with *line control discipline; line discipline.*

prototype: in expert systems development, an initial version of an expert system, usually a system with from 25 to 200 rules, that is devel-

147

oped to test effectiveness of the overall knowledge representation and inference strategies being employed to solve a specific problem.

prototype development: the third phase in knowledge engineering; involves the development of a small version of the expert system to demonstrate feasibility and to experiment with the various problems to be encountered when full-scale development is undertaken. For other phases see *knowledge engineering.*

proximal: close to the base, away from the end effector of the arm.

proximity sensors: units for sensing that an object is only a short distance (e.g., a few inches or feet) away, and/or measuring how far away it is, working on the principles of triangulation of reflected light, lapsed time for reflected sound, and others.

pruning: in expert systems, the process whereby one or more branches of a decision tree are "cut off" or ignored. In effect, when an expert system consultation is under way, heuristic rules reduce the search space by determining that certain branches (or subsets of rules) can be ignored.

PS: see *picosecond.*

pseudocode: a code that requires translation prior to execution.

pseudorandom number sequence: an ordered set of numbers that has been determined by some defined arithmetic process, but which is effectively a random number sequence for the specific purpose for which it is required.

PSI: an expert system that converts English language specifications into simple programs.

PSL: see *portable standard LISP.*

PSM: a procedural semantic network for a knowledge base using classes, objects, and relations.

PUFF: an expert system for assisting in the diagnosis of respiratory diseases.

pulse generator: a device for generating electronic pulses.

punched card: a card punched with hole patterns. see *Hollerith card.*

punched tape: a tape punched with hole patterns. synonymous with *perforated tape.*

pure binary numeration system: the fixed-radix numeration system that uses the binary digits and the radix 2; for example, in this numeration system, the numeral 110.01 represents the number "six and one

148

quarter," that is, $1 \times 2^2 + 1 \times 2^1 + 1 \times 2^{-2}$. synonymous with *binary numeration system*.

PUSH: slang; to place information into the stack.

push-down list: a list that is constructed and maintained so that the next item to be retrieved and removed is the most recently stored item still in the list, that is, last-in, first out (LIFO). synonymous with *stack*.

push-up list: a list that is constructed and maintained so that the next item to be retrieved is the earliest stored item still in the list, that is, first-in, first-out (FIFO).

Q

(1)   see *query*.

(2)   see *quotient*.

QT: see *quotient*.

quantization: the subdivision of the range of values of a variable into a finite number of nonoverlapping, and not necessarily equal subranges or intervals, each of which is represented by an assigned value within the subrange; for example, a person's age is quantized for most purposes with a quantum of one year.

quantize: to divide the range of a variable into a finite number of nonoverlapping intervals that are not necessarily equal, and to designate each interval by an assigned value within that interval.

quartet: a byte composed of four binary elements. synonymous with *four-bit byte*.

query (Q)

(1)   the process by which a master station asks a slave station to identify itself and to give its status.

(2)   in interactive systems, an operation at a terminal that elicits a response from the system.

query language: synonymous with *command language*.

queuing: the programming technique used to handle messages awaiting transmission.

quintet: a byte composed of five binary elements. synonymous with *five-bit byte*.

QUIP: an experimental work station for geologists, oriented toward enabling quick testing of geological and rock models.

quotient (Q) (QT):   the number or quantity that is the value of the dividend divided by the value of the divisor and which is one of the results of a division operation.

R

R
(1) see *register*.
(2) see *relation*.

RAA: see *remote axis admittance*.

radix: in a radix numeration system, the positive integer by which the weight of the digit place is multiplied to obtain the weight of the digit place with the next higher weight; for example, in the decimal numeration system the radix of each digit place is 10, in a biquinary code the radix of each fives position is 2. see *floating-point base*.

radix complement (RC): a complement obtained by subtracting each digit of the given number from the number that is one less than the radix of that digit place, then adding one to the least significant digit of the result and executing any carries required; for example, 830 is the tens complement (i.e., the radix complement of 170 in the decimal numeration system using three digits). synonymous with *noughts complement; true complement.*

radix notation: synonymous with *radix numeration system.*

radix numeration system: a positional representation system in which the ratio of the weight of any one digit place to the weight of the digit place with the next lower weight is a positive integer. The permissible values of the character in any digit place range from zero to one less than the radix of that digit place. synonymous with *radix notation.*

radix point: in a representation of a number expressed in a radix numeration system, the location of the separation of the characters associated with the integral part from those associated with the fractional part.

RAIL: a computer language for robots.

RAM: random-access memory. The most common computer memory, the contents of which can be altered at any time.

RAMUS: a modern, sophisticated language for data base interaction.

random access

(1)   a method of providing or achieving access whereby the time to retrieve data is constant and independent of the location of the item addressed previously.

(2)   in COBOL, an access mode in which specific logic records are obtained from or placed into a mass storage file in a nonsequential manner.

random-access memory: see *RAM.*

random-access storage: a storage unit such as magnetic core, magnetic disk, and magnetic drum in which each record has a specific predetermined address that may be reached directly. synonymous with *direct-access storage.*

random file: data records stored in a file without regard to the sequences of the key or control field.

random number

(1)   a number selected from a known set of numbers in such a way that the probability of occurrence of each number in the set is equal.

(2)   a number obtained by chance.

(3)   one of a sequence of numbers considered appropriate for satisfying certain statistical tests.

(4)   one of a sequence of numbers believed to be free from conditions that might bias the result of a calculation.

range-imaging sensors: sensors that measure the distance from themselves to a raster of points in the scene; applied primarily to object recognition. Useful in finding a factory floor or road, detecting obstacles and pits, and inspecting the completeness of subassemblies.

raster: in computer graphics, a predetermined pattern of lines that provides uniform coverage of a display space.

rate control: a control system in which the input is the desired velocity of the controlled object.

rated load capacity: a particular weight or mass of a material that is handled by a machine or process permitting for some margin of safety relative to the point of expected failure.

rational number: a real number that is the quotient of an integer divided by an integer other than zero.

RC: see *radix complement.*

RCC: see *remote center compliance.*

reach: pertaining to the robot's arm movement or work envelope. The work envelope has one of three shapes—cylindrical, spherical, or spheroidal—with three major parameters: (1) degrees of rotation about the center axis (horizontal arm sweep), (2) vertical motion at both minimum and maximum arm extension, and (3) radial arm extension, measured from the center axis.

read-around ratio: the number of times a specific spot, digit, or location in electrostatic storage may be consulted before spillover of electrons causes a loss of data stored in surrounding spots. The surrounding data must be restored before the deterioration results in any loss of data.

read-eval-print loop: in LISP, the EVAL function, when called, effects a read-eval-print loop; where a form is given to an interpreter, the form is evaluated, and a value is returned which is usually displayed.

read-in: to sense information contained in some source and to transfer this information by means of an input unit to internal storage.

read-only memory (ROM): possessing a space of 1024 eight-bit data units. Once bits are stored in ROM they cannot be erased and will not disappear when the power running the computer is turned off. They are prefabricated circuitry and are needed in a unit. Their configuration cannot be altered in computer operation. Generally ROM carries the basic instructions for controlling a robot. synonymous with *fixed storage.*

read-only storage (ROS): special circuitry in a computer permitting it to process commands written for other computers. Some new computers use ROS as an integral part of their own command circuitry. synonymous with *permanent storage.*

read-out: a display of processed information on a terminal screen.

read/write head: synonymous with *magnetic head.*

real constant: a string of decimal digits that must have either a decimal point or a decimal exponent, and which may have both.

real number: a number that may be represented by a finite or infinite numeral in a fixed-radix numeration system.

real time (RT)

(1) pertaining to the processing of data by a computer in connection with another process outside the computer. This is dependent on time requirements imposed by the outside printing of conversational modes and processes, which can be influenced by human intervention while they are in progress.

(2) pertaining to an application in which response to input is fast enough

to affect subsequent input, such as a process control system or a computer-assisted instruction system.

real-world problem: a complex, practical problem having a solution that is useful in some cost-effective fashion.

reasoning: the process of drawing inferences or conclusions.

reason maintenance: the process of keeping track of the dependencies between assertions in a knowledge base for assisting in the making and withdrawing of deductions as new information becomes available.

recency: a conflict-resolution strategy favoring instantiations whose working memory elements were most recently created or modified, lending sensitivity to a production system, since subgoals can be spawned as soon as new data arrives.

recognize-act cycle: the cycle of events in a production or forward-chaining system. During the recognize phase, rules are examined to see if their *if* clauses are true, based on information currently stored in memory. During the act phase, one of the rules is chosen and executed and its conclusion is stored in memory.

recording density: the number of bits in a single linear track, measured per unit of length of the recording medium.

record-playback robot: a robot where the critical points along preferred trajectories are stored in sequence by recording the actual values of the joint-position encoders of the robot during movement under operator control.

rectangular coordinate system: synonymous with *Cartesian coordinate system*.

rectilinear-Cartesian robot: a continuous-path, extended-reach robot providing the flexibility and versatility of multiple robots. It utilizes a bridge and trolley construction, enabling it to have a large rectangular work envelope.

rectilinear-coordinate robot: a robot placed on a fixed base where all arm motions of the manipulator are in a straight line; either in–out, up–down, or side–to–side.

recursive: pertaining to a process in which each step makes use of the results of earlier steps.

recursive function: a function whose values are natural numbers that are derived from natural numbers by substitution formulae in which the function is an operand.

156

redundancy

(1) in information theory, the amount R by which the decision content H_0 exceeds the entropy H; in mathematical notation, $R = H_0 - H$. Usually, messages can be represented with fewer characters by using suitable codes; the redundancy may be considered as a measure of the decrease of length of the messages thus achieved.

(2) in the transmission of information, that fraction of the gross information content of a message that can be eliminated without loss of essential information.

reenterable program: synonymous with *reentrant program.*

reentrant program: a computer program that may be entered repeatedly and which may be entered before prior executions of the same computer program have been completed, subject to the requirement that neither its external program parameters nor any instructions are modified during its execution. A reentrant program may be used by more than one computer program simultaneously. synonymous with *reenterable program.*

reflected binary code: synonymous with *gray code.*

refraction: a conflict-resolution strategy preventing an instantiation from firing, should it have fired on an earlier occasion.

refreshable: the attribute of a load module that prevents it from being modified by itself or by another module during execution. A refreshable load module can be replaced by a new copy during execution by a recovery management routine without changing either the sequence or results of processing.

REG: see *register.*

regenerative track: part of a track on a magnetic drum or magnetic disk used in conjunction with a read head and a write head that are connected to function as a circulating storage. synonymous with *revolver track.*

REGIS: see *register.*

register (R) (REG) (REGIS)

(1) a storage device having a specified storage capacity such as a bit, a byte, or a computer word, and usually intended for a special purpose.

(2) a part of an automatic switching system that receives and stores signals from a calling device or other source for interpretation and action, some of which is carried out by the register itself.

relation (R): in assembler programming, the comparison of two expres-

157

sions to see if the value of one is equal to, less than, or greater than the value of the other.

relation address: an address expressed as a difference with respect to a base address.

relative character: in COBOL, a character that expresses a relationship between two operands.

relative command: in computer graphics, a display command that causes the display device to interpret the data following the order as relative coordinates, rather than absolute coordinates. synonymous with *relative order.*

relative coordinate: in computer graphics, one of the coordinates that identify the location of an addressable point by means of a displacement from some other addressable point.

relative data: in computer graphics, values in a computer program that specify displacements from the actual coordinates in a display space or image space.

relative error: the ratio of an absolute error to the true, specified, or theoretically correct value of the quantity that is in error.

relative order: synonymous with *relative command.*

reliability: the ability of a function unit to perform its intended function under stated conditions, for a stated period of time.

relocation factor: the algebraic difference between the assembled origin and the loaded origin of a computer program.

remote axis admittance (RAA): a unit that performs the fine motions of parts mating, that can be mounted on the end of a robot arm, and that will perform the final phases of assembly when the parts are in close proximity and in contact. The RAA can be adapted to a number of different types of tasks, including simple insertion, such as the chamfered peg and hole, the insertion of edges in slots, the multiple insertion, and the chamferless insertion. The RAA can be used together with different types of robot arms to perform parts fetching and assembly.

remote batch processing: batch processing in which input/output units have access to a computer through a data link.

remote center compliance (RCC): a compliant unit for interfacing a robot or other mechanical workhead to its tool or working medium by permitting a gripped part to rotate about its tip, or to translate without rotating when pushed laterally at its tip. The RCC provides general lateral and rotational float and greatly eases robot or other mechanical assembly in the presence of errors in parts, jigs, pallets, and robots. It is particularly useful in performing very close clearance or interference insertions.

remote job entry (RJE):   submission of jobs through an input unit that has access to a computer through a data link.

repeatability

(1) *computers:* the measure of the difference between the mean value and some maximum expected value for a particular data reading.

(2) *robotics:* the closeness of agreement of repeated position movement, under identical conditions, to the same location.

repetitive addressing: a method of implied addressing, applicable only to zero-address instructions, in which the operation part of an instruction implicitly addresses the operands of the last instruction executed.

replica master: a teleoperator control device that is kinematically equivalent to the slave manipulator or other unit that is being controlled (e.g., the master has the same kind of joints in the same relative positions as does the slave). A replica master can be larger than, smaller than, or the same size as the slave unit it controls, having or not having a geometry similar to that of a human arm.

report generator: a general-purpose program designed to print out information from files when presented with parameters specifying the format of the files concerned, plus the format and content of the printed report, and procedures and regulations for establishing totals, page numbering, and so on. synonymous with *program generator.*

representation: the formalization and structuring of knowledge in a computer so that it can be manipulated by the knowledge base management system.

reprogrammable: pertaining to a computer program that can be changed.

reserved word

(1) a word of a source language whose meaning is fixed by the particular rules of that language, and which cannot be altered for the convenience of any one computer program expressed in the source language. Computer programs expressed in the source language may also be prohibited from using such words in other contexts in the computer program; for example, SINE may be a reserved word to call a subroutine for computing the sine function; in COBOL, the COBOL words are reserved.

(2) a word that is defined in a programming language for a special purpose, and that must not appear as user-declared identifier.

residue check: a validation check in which an operand is divided by a number to generate a remainder that is then used for checking. synonymous with *modulo-N check.*

resolution

(1) *general:* the inference strategy used in logic systems to determine the truth of an assertion. This complex, but highly effective, method established the truth of an assertion by determining that a contradiction is encountered when one attempts to resolve clauses, one of which is a negation of the thesis one seeks. synonymous with *resolution theorem proving.*

(2) *computer graphics:* a measure of the sharpness of an image, expressed as the number of lines per unit of length, or the number of points per unit of area discernible in that image.

(3) *robotics:* the smallest interval between two adjacent discrete details that can be distinguished.

(4) *robotics:* the smallest increment of distance that can be read and acted upon by an automatic control system.

resolution theorem-proving: synonymous with *resolution (1).*

resolved motion rate control: a control technique whereby the velocity vector of the end point of a manipulator arm is commanded and the computer determines the joint angular velocities to achieve the desired result. Coordination of a robot's axes so that the velocity vector of the end joint is under direct control. Motion in the coordinate system of the end point along specified directions or trajectories is possible. Used in manual control of manipulators, and as a computational method for achieving programmed coordinate axis control in robots.

resolver

(1) *computers:* a functional unit whose input variables are the polar coordinates of a point and whose output variables are the Cartesian coordinates of the same point, or vice versa.

(2) *robotics:* a rotary or linear feedback unit for converting mechanical motion to analog electric signals that represent motion or position.

Rete match algorithm: an algorithm for efficiently determining which rules can be satisfied by the contents of working memory (on each recognize-act cycle) by computing bindings between patterns and data.

retrieve: synonymous with *fetch.*

return-to-reference recording: the magnetic recording of binary characters in which the patterns of magnetization used to represent zeros and ones occupy only part of the storage cell, the remainder of the cell being magnetized to a reference condition.

reverse Polish notation: synonymous with *postfix notation.*

revolver track: synonymous with *regenerative track.*

REX: a regression expert; a frame-based expert system that does statistical analysis.

RHS: see *right-hand side.*

right-hand side (RHS): one of the two parts of a rule. In production systems with backward-chaining architecture, specifies a goal to be solved, the subgoals of which are given on the left-hand side of the rule. In forward-chaining production systems, consists of a series of actions to be performed in a specified sequence when an instantiation of the rule is fired, using values that were bound to variables on the left-hand side. cf. *left-hand side.*

right memory: a data structure in the Rete match algorithm network associated with a condition element; contains a list of working memory elements that match the condition.

RJE: see *remote job entry.*

robot

(1) a machine equipped with sensing instruments for detecting input signals or environmental conditions, but with reacting or guidance mechanisms that can perform sensing, calculations, and so on, and with stored programs for resultant actions; for example, a machine running itself.

(2) a mechanical unit that can be programmed to perform some task of manipulation or locomotion under automatic control.

robotics: an area of artificial intelligence applied to the industrial use of robots for performing repetitive tasks.

robotics science: the science of connection perception to action through intelligent programs.

robotnik: the original Czech term for robot, meaning "slave."

robot programming language: a computer language designed for the creation of programs to be used for controlling robots.

robot system: includes the robot hardware and software, consisting of the manipulator, power supply, and controller; the end effector(s); any equipment, devices, and sensors the robot is directly interfacing with;

any equipment, devices, and sensors required for the robot to perform its task; and any communications interface that is operating and monitoring the robot, equipment, and sensors.

robustness: a quality of a problem solver permitting a gradual degradation in performance when it is pushed to the limits of its scope of expertise or is given errorful, inconsistent, or incomplete data or rules.

rod memory: a thin-film memory in which metallic film is deposited on short metallic rods. The rods are then strung into planes and stacked according to the coding structure of the system.

roll: see *wrist movement.*

ROM: see *read-only memory.*

R1: synonymous with *XCON.* see also *OPS.*

root segment

(1) in an overlay program, the segment that remains in storage during the execution of the overlay program; the first segment in an overlay program.

(2) in a data base, the highest segment in the hierarchy.

ROS: see *read-only storage.*

rotation: the movement of a body around an axis in such a way that (at least) one point remains fixed.

rote learning: learning by direct memorization of facts, without generalization. see also *caching.*

round: to delete or omit one or more of the least significant digits in order to limit the precision of the numeral or to reduce the number of characters in the numeral, or to do both.

routing

(1) *computers:* the assignment of the path by which a message will reach its destination.

(2) *production:* the sequence of operations to be performed in order to produce a part or an assembly.

row binary: pertaining to the binary representation of data on cards on which the significances of punch positions are assigned along card rows; for example, each row in an 80-column card may be used to represent 80 consecutive binary digits. cf. *column binary.*

RPL: a robot programming language.

RS-232-C, RS-422, RS-423, RS-449: standard electrical interfaces for connecting peripheral units to computers. Standard RS-449, together with standard RS-422 and RS-423, is replacing the widely used RS-

232-C as the specification for the interface between data terminal equipment and data circuit-terminating equipment employing serial binary data interchange. Compatible with devices using RS-232-C, RS-449 takes advantage of advances in integrated circuit design, reduces crosstalk between interchange circuits, allows greater distance between devices, and permits higher data signaling rates (up to 2 million bits per second). RS-449 specifies functional and mechanical aspects of the interface, such as the use of two connectors having 37 pins and 9 pins, instead of a single 25-pin connector. RS-422 specifies the electrical aspects for wideband communication over balanced lines at data rates up to 10 million bits per second. RS-423 does the same for unbalanced lines at data rates up to 100,000 bits per second.

RT: see *real time.*

rule: a formal way of specifying a recommendation, directive, or strategy, expressed as IF premise THEN conclusion or IF condition THEN action. Sometimes called *situation-action pairs.* see also *if-then rule.*

rule-based methods: programming techniques using if-then rules to perform forward or backward chaining.

rule-based system: a system where knowledge is stored in the form of simple if-then or condition-action rules.

rule cluster: rules that work together to achieve a goal, or the set of rules related to a context element.

rule filtering: limiting (for the sake of efficiency) the portion of production memory that participates in the match process to a subset.

rule interpreter: in production systems, synonymous with *interpreter.*

RuleMaster: a combination induction and rule-based tool derived from the conceptual approach to expert system tool design; written in C and will run in most UNIX environments. The tool has the feel of a conventional programming language, rather than of a friendly rule-based tool such as EMYCIN. see also *C.*

rule memory: synonymous with *production memory.*

run-length encoding: a data compression method for reducing the amount of information in a digitized binary image. It removes the redundancy that arises from the fact that such images have large regions of adjacent pixels that are either all white or all black.

runtime system (version): knowledge system building tools that allow the user to create and run various knowledge bases. Using a single tool, a user can create a dozen knowledge bases. For example, depending on the problem the user was facing, he or she would load an appropriate knowledge base and undertake a consultation. With such a tool the user can easily modify a knowledge base. When an expert system building tool is modified to incorporate a specific knowledge base and to deactivate certain programming features, the resulting system is called a *runtime system* or *runtime version*.

S

S

(1)   see *software*.

(2)   see *switch*.

SAM: see *sequential-access memory*.

satisfice: a process during which one seeks a solution that will satisfy a set of constraints. In contrast to optimization, which seeks the best possible solution, when one satisfices, one simply seeks a solution that will work.

saturation

(1)   the condition of magnetism of a material beyond which no additional magnetization is possible.

(2)   a range within which output is constant regardless of input.

scalar: in programming languages, one of the primitive data types, usually an integer, floating-point number, character, logical value, or symbolic atom, but not a list, array, or record.

scale

(1)   to change the representation of a quantity by expressing it in other units, so that its range is brought within a specified range.

(2)   to adjust the representation of a quantity by a factor, in order to bring its range within prescribed limits.

(3)   in computer graphics, to enlarge or reduce all or part of a display image by multiplying their coordinate by constant values.

(4)   a system of mathematical notation (e.g., a fixed-point or floating-point scale of an arithmetic value).

scaling

(1)   in computer graphics, enlarging or reducing all or part of a display image by multiplying the coordinates of the image by a constant value.

(2)   in assembler programming, indicating the number of digit positions in object code to be occupied by the fractional portion of a fixed-point or floating-point constant.

scanner (SCN):   a device that examines a spatial pattern one part after another, and generates analog or digital signals corresponding to the pattern. Scanners are often used in mark sensing, pattern recognition, or character recognition. see *flying spot scanner; optical scanner.*

SCARA: selective compliance assembly robot arm. A robot with four axes: two planar articulated motions of the arm and two wrist motions.

schema: a symbolic structure that is filled with specific information for denoting an instance of the generic concept represented by the structure.

scheme representation language: see *SRL.*

SCN: see *scanner.*

scope (scoping):   in a program, the extent to which a variable is bound (defined); for example, local variables are bound only within the mode that gets executed during a function call.

SCR: see *silicon-controlled rectifier.*

scroll

(1)   to move all or part of the display image vertically to display data that cannot be observed within a single display image.

(2)   a graphic display technique whereby the generation of a new line of alphanumeric text at the bottom of a display screen automatically regenerates all other lines of text one line higher than before and deletes the top line.

(3)   in computer graphics, the continuous vertical or horizontal movement of the display elements within a window in a manner such that new data appear at one edge of the window as old data disappear at the opposite edge. The window may include the entire display surface.

SDLC: see *synchronous data link control.*

search function: where a robot system adjusts the position of data points within an existing cycle based on changes in external equipment and workpieces.

search language: synonymous with *command language.*

search space: see *problem space.*

second-generation computer: a computer utilizing solid-state components.

section

(1)   in COBOL, a logically related sequence of one or more paragraphs. A section must always be named.

(2)   in computer graphics, to construct a bounded or unbounded inter-

166

secting plane with respect to one or more displayed objects, and then to display the intersection.

segmentation: a programmer-defined and monitor-implemented approach of separating a program into self-contained segments so that only certain parts need be in memory at any one time.

segment variable: a variable in a pattern that matches a subpart of a list.

selective compliance assembly robot arm: see *SCARA*.

self-replication: to produce a copy of oneself.

semantic: the meaning of an expression. cf. *syntactic*.

semantic networks: a form of knowledge representation that formalizes objects and values as nodes, and connects the nodes with arcs or links that indicate the relationships between the various nodes.

sensitivity: the responsiveness of a system to the dynamically altering demands of its environment.

sensor: a device that converts measurable elements of a physical process into data meaningful to a computer.

sensors, contact: see *contact sensor*.

sensors, electrooptical imaging: see *electrooptical imaging sensors*.

sensors, force and torque: see *force and torque sensors*.

sensors, photoelectric proximity (noncontact): see *photoelectric proximity (noncontact) sensors*.

sensors, proximity (noncontact): see *proximity (noncontact) sensors*.

sensors, range-imaging: see *range-imaging sensors*.

sensors, touch: see *touch sensors*.

sensors, vision: see *vision sensors*.

sensors, wrist force: see *wrist force sensors*.

sensory control: the control of a robot based on sensor readings. Used for terminating robot activity or for branching to another activity, for guiding or directing changes in robot motions, for monitoring robot progress and checking for task completion or unsafe conditions, and for retrospectively updating robot motion plans prior to the following cycle.

sensory-controlled robot: a robot whose control is a function of information sensed from its environment.

sensory hierarchy: the relationship of sensory processing elements whereby the results of lower-level elements are used as inputs by higher-level elements.

sentinel: synonymous with *flag*.

separating character: synonymous with *information separator.*

sequence checking: used to prove that a set of data is arranged in either ascending or descending order prior to processing.

sequence codes: in sequence coding, numbers are assigned to a list of items in a straight sequence—starting with one—without concern for the classification or order of the subjects being coded. It is useful for any short list of names, products, or accounts where the only object is the application of simple code numbers, and where the arrangement of data is not important.

sequence control register: synonymous with *instruction address register.*

sequence robot: a robot whose motion trajectory follows a preset sequence of positional changes.

sequencing: ordering in a series or according to rank or time.

sequential-access memory (SAM): an auxiliary memory unit, lacking any addressable data areas. A specific piece of data can only be found by means of a sequential search through the file.

sequential batch processing: a mode of operating a computer in which one run must be completed before another run can be started.

sequential control: a mode of computer operation in which instructions are executed in an implicitly defined sequence until a different sequence is explicitly initiated by a jump instruction.

SER: see *serial.*

serial (SER)

(1) pertaining to the sequential performance of two or more activities in a single device. In English, the modifiers serial and parallel usually refer to devices, as opposed to sequential and consecutive, which refer to processes.

(2) pertaining to the sequential or consecutive occurrence of two or more related activities in a single device or channel.

(3) pertaining to the sequential processing of the individual parts of a whole such as the bits of a character or the characters of a word, using the same facilities for successive parts. cf. *parallel.*

serial arithmetic operations: a means by which the computer handles arithmetic fields one digit at a time, usually from right to left.

serial communications: a digital communication method for transmitting the bits of a message one at a time; the most common long-

168

distance transmission method; suitable for use with cable, radio, or modulated light as the transmission medium.

serial operation: pertaining to the sequential or consecutive execution of two or more operations in a single device such as an arithmetic or logic unit.

service program: synonymous with *utility program.*

servo-control approach: see *continuous-path control.*

servo-controlled robot: a robot possessing smooth motions with speed and (often) acceleration and deceleration controlled, allowing for heavy load movement. Flexibility is determined by programming the axes of the manipulator to any position within limits of their travel. Unreliable at times, these robots are often used to maintain nonservo robots, which are usually less costly.

servomechanism

(1) an automatic device that uses feedback to govern the physical position of an element.

(2) a feedback control system in which at least one of the system signals represents mechanical motion.

servovalve: a transducer whose input is a low-energy signal, and whose output is a higher-energy fluid flow that is proportional to the low-energy signal.

sexadecimal

(1) pertaining to a selection, choice, or condition that has 16 possible different values or states.

(2) pertaining to a fixed-radix numeration system having a radix of 16. synonymous with *hexadecimal.*

S-expression: symbolic expression. In LISP, a list. Beginning with a left parenthesis, containing functions, atoms, or sublists and ending with a balancing right parenthesis.

shaft encoder: an encoder used for measuring shaft position.

Shakey: a robot developed at Stanford University in 1969.

Shannon: in information theory, a unit of logarithmic measures of information equal to the decision content of a set of two mutually exclusive events expressed by the logarithm to base two; for example, the decision content of a character set of eight characters equals three Shannons. synonymous with *information content binary unit.*

shared control: a facility that permits multiple concurrent interactions with a specific unit of data in a data base.

Sheffer stroke: synonymous with *NAND*.

shell: in software, particularly in UNIX, a program that runs on top of an operating system which aids in using the operating system and provides an interface to higher-level programs such as tools and applications.

short-term memory: that portion of human memory that is actively used when we think about a problem. By analogy to a computer, it is like RAM; it contains all the data that is instantly available to the system. Its content is conceptualized in terms of chunks. Most cognitive theories hold that human short-term memory can contain and manipulate about four chunks at one time. synonymous with *working memory*.

short-term repeatability: the closeness of agreement of position movements, repeated under the same conditions during a short time interval, to the same location.

shoulder: the manipulator joint located between the base and the upper arm.

side effect: in LISP, action returned by a call function in addition to a value.

sign bit: a bit or a binary element that occupies a sign position and indicates the algebraic sign of the number represented by the numeral with which it is associated.

sign character: a character that occupies a sign position and indicates the algebraic sign of the number represented by the numeral with which it is associated.

significance: synonymous with *weight*.

significant digit: in a numeral, a digit that is needed for a given purpose; in particular, a digit that must be kept to preserve a given accuracy or precision.

significant digit arithmetic: a method of making calculations using a modified form of a floating-point representation system in which the number of significant digits in the result is determined with reference to the number of significant digits in the operands, the operation performed, and the degree of precision available.

significant digit codes: coding where all or part of the numbers are related to some characteristic of the data (e.g., weight, dimension, distance, capacity, etc.), thereby reducing the work of decoding by providing a code number that can be read directly.

silicon-controlled rectifier (SCR): a three-junction rectifying unit that is triggered by means of a specified voltage applied to a gate terminal.

170

SIM: see *simulator.*

similarity metric

(1) a context-free mathematical measure of properties of object descriptions used in clustering—minimized for objects within a cluster, and maximized for objects spanning clusters.

(2) a context-sensitive symbolic expression capturing relevant similarities between two object or process descriptions; used to establish mappings in analogical inference. see *analogical inference.*

SIMULA: one of the first object-oriented programming languages, originally intended for simulation work.

simulator (SIM): a device, data processing system, or computer program that represents certain features of the behavior of a physical or abstract system.

simultaneous computer: a computer that contains a separate unit to perform each portion of the entire computation concurrently, the units being interconnected in a way determined by the computation. At different times in a run, a given interconnection carries signals representing different values of the same variable; for example, a differential analyzer.

situation: a state of data memory corresponding to some set of properties in the domain being modeled by the production system. Rules are sometimes called *situation-action pairs.*

situation-action pairs: see *rules.* see also *situation.*

skeletal code: a set of instructions in which some parts such as addresses must be completed or specified in detail each time the set is used.

SKETCHPAD: an early experimental system for computer-aided design.

skill: the efficient and effective application of knowledge for producing solutions in a problem domain.

skill acquisition (and refinement): acquiring or improving a procedural skill by knowledge compilation and repeated practice. see *knowledge compilation.*

slew rate: the maximum velocity at which a manipulator joint can move; the rate imposed by saturation somewhere in the servo loop controlling that joint (e.g., by a value's reaching its maximum open-setting). The maximum speed at which the tool tip can move in an inertial Cartesian frame.

slot: a component of an object in a frame system. Slots can contain intrinsic features such as the object's name, attributes and values, attributes with default values, rules to determine values, pointers to related frames, information about the frame's creator, and so on.

small knowledge system: a system containing fewer than 500 rules; designed to help people solve different analysis and decision-making tasks without aspiring to being the equivalent of any human expert.

small knowledge system building tools: tools that can run on personal computers.

SMALLTALK: a programming language that popularized a style of programming according to which procedures communicate by sending each other messages. SMALLTALK is particularly effective with graphics-oriented programming.

smart sensor: a sensing unit whose output signal is contingent on mathematical or logical operations and inputs other than from the sensor itself.

SNOBOL: see *String Oriented Symbolic Language.*

SOFT: see *software.*

soft automation: see *hard automation.*

software (S) (SOFT) (SW): programs, procedures, rules, and any associated documentation pertaining to the operation of a computer system.

software engineer: a person who designs conventional computer software, serving a role similar to a knowledge engineer in the development of a conventional software program.

software engineering: synonymous with *programming.*

solenoid: a switch that functions based on the principles of electromagnetism. A current passes through a coil that is built around an armature, which moves under the influence of the current to open or close a contact.

solid-state camera: a TV camera using some type of solid-state integrated circuit instead of a vacuum tube to change a light image into a video signal.

SOM: see *start-of-message code.*

SOPHIE: an experimental instruction system that teaches students how to debug electronic circuits.

source code file: in software, a file containing a program.

source document: a form containing data that are eventually processed by a computer.

source file: see *source code file.*

source language: a language from which statements are translated.

source program: a computer program expressed in a source language. cf. *target program.*

SP: see *space character.*

space character (SP): a graphic character that is usually represented by a blank site in a series of graphics. The space character, though not a control character, has a function equivalent to that of a format effector that causes the print or display position to move one position forward without producing the printing or display of any graphic. Similarly, the space character may have a function equivalent to that of an information separator. see also *null character.*

specialization: narrowing the scope of a concept description, thereby reducing the sets of instances it describes. see *concept description.*

special purpose robot: a robot with considerable versatility that can readily be changed over, installed, and maintained.

specific address: synonymous with *absolute address.*

specificity: a conflict resolution strategy that prefers instantiations of more specific rules, usually measured in terms of numbers of variables and constants, or numbers of left-hand-side tests.

speech recognition: the ability of a computer to respond to speech patterns.

speech synthesis: the production of speech by computer.

speech understanding: the use of AI techniques to process and interpret audio signals representing human speech.

speed: the maximum speed at which a robot moves. Usually, the maximum tool tip speed in an inertial reference frame.

spherical-coordinate robot: a rotary based robot with an arm that can extend and retract, and be pivoted to swing vertically, permitting rotary motion about a horizontal plane.

spherical coordinate system: a coordinate system, two of whose dimensions are angles, the third being a linear distance from the point of origin. These three coordinates specify a point on a sphere.

spreading activation: in an activation network, a means of altering the pattern of activation or attention in the network so that activation flows outward from active nodes, activating nodes that are connected directly or indirectly.

springback: the deflection of a body when external load is removed; usually, the deflection of the end effector of a manipulator arm.

SRL: scheme representation language, a program used for knowledge description.

stability: continuity of behavior of a system. In a production system, stability is influenced by its conflict resolution strategy.

stable state: in a trigger circuit, a state in which the circuit remains until the application of a suitable pulse.

stack: synonymous with *push-down list*.

staging: the moving of data from an office or low-priority device back to an on-line or higher-priority device, usually on demand of the system or on request of the user.

standard binary-coded-decimal interchange code: a computer code in most second-generation computers which is an expansion of the binary-coded-decimal system. The significant difference in the standard BCD code is the use of zone bits. The zone bits of an alphanumeric character perform a code function similar to the zone positions of a punched card. They are used in combination with digits to represent the letters of the alphabet or special characters.

standard branching: a way for industrial robot systems to select or alter the programmed path and function based on changes in the environment around them. The robot reaches some point and interrogates an input signal to determine whether it is electrically active, or the robot is interrupted by activation of another input signal. The robot path then branches to a section of the path/function programs; if no signal is present at this decision point, or no interrupt occurs, the robot continues in a normal path sequence.

standing-on-nines carry: in the parallel addition of numbers represented by decimal numerals, a procedure in which a carry to a given digit place is bypassed to the next digit place. If the current sum in the given digit place is nine, the nine is changed to zero.

start-of-message (SOM) code: a character or group of characters transmitted by the polled terminal indicating to other stations on the line that what follows are addresses of key stations to receive the answering message.

statement
    (1) in a programming language, a meaningful expression that may

describe or specify operations and is usually complete in the context of that programming language.

(2)   in computer programming, a symbol string or other arrangement of symbols.

(3)   in COBOL, a syntactically valid combination of words and symbols written in the procedure division. A statement combines COBOL reserved words and programmer-defined operands.

(4)   in FORTRAN, the basic unit of a program, composed of a line or lines containing some combination of names, operators, constants, or words whose meaning is predefined to the FORTRAN compiler. Statements fall into two broad classes: executable and nonexecutable.

(5)   a basic element of a PL/1 program that is used to delimit a portion of the program, to describe names used in the program, or to specify action to be taken. A statement can consist of a condition list, a label list, a statement identifier, and a statement body that is terminated by a semicolon.

static accuracy: the deviation from time value when relevant variables are not changing with time. The difference between actual position response and position desired or commanded of an automatic control system as determined in the steady state; that is, when all transient responses have died out.

station control: a module in a control hierarchy that controls a work station. The station control module is controlled by a cell control module.

steady state: a condition where all values remain essentially constant or recur in a cyclic fashion.

STEAMER: an experimental instruction system that teaches propulsion engineering (featuring sophisticated procedures for graphics-oriented simulation) and qualitative reasoning.

stepper motor: an electric motor whose windings are arranged in such a way that the armature can be made to step in discrete rotational increments when a digital pulse is applied to an accompanying driver circuit. The armature displacement stays locked in this angular position, independent of applied torque, up to a limit. synonymous with *stepping motor.*

stepping motor: synonymous with *stepper motor.*

stepwise refinement: synonymous with *top-down programming.*

stiction: statis friction, the force that prevents two mated surfaces from moving relative to one another.

stop: a mechanical restraint or limit on some motion that is set to stop the motion at a desired point.

storage tube: in computer graphics, a type of cathode-ray tube (CRT) that retains a display image on its screen for an extended period of time without requiring refresh.

stored program computer: a computer having the ability to store, refer to, and modify instruction in directing its step-by-step operations.

straight-line coding

(1) a set of instructions in which there are no loops.

(2) a programming technique in which loops are avoided by unwinding.

strain gage (gauge)

(1) a sensor producing voltage or resistance change when a force is present.

(2) a sensor that, when cemented to elastic materials, measures very small amounts of stretch by the change in the material's electrical resistance. When used on materials with high modulus of elasticity, strain gages become force sensors.

strain gage (gauge) rosette: multiple strain gages cemented in two- or three-dimensional geometric patterns such that independent measurements of the strain of each can be combined to yield a vector measurement of strain or force.

stratified language: a language that cannot be used as its own metalanguage; for example, FORTRAN. cf. *unstratified language.*|

string: a linear sequence of entities such as characters or physical elements. see *alphabetic string; bit string.*

String Oriented Symbolic Language (SNOBOL): a high-level programming language oriented toward the maneuvering of character strings.

stroke edge: in character recognition, the line of discontinuity between the side of a stroke and the background. It is obtained by averaging, over the length of the stroke, the irregularities resulting from the printing and detecting processes.

structural description: a symbolic representation of objects and concepts, based on descriptions of their parts and the relationships among them.

structural similarity: in a production system, the syntactic commonalities among rules that have identical values for attributes, identical condition elements, or sequences of identical condition elements which are structurally similar.

structured programming: a technique for organizing and coding programs that reduces complexity, improves clarity, and makes them easier to debug and modify. Typically, a structured program is a hierarchy of modules that each have a single entry point and a single exit point; control is passed downward through the structure without unconditional branches to higher levels of the structure. synonymous with *GOTO-less programming.*

structure light: illumination created so that the three-dimensional pattern of light energy in the viewing volumes causes visible patterns to appear on the surface of objects being viewed, from which patterns that are the shape of the objects can easily be determined.

SUB: see *subroutine.*

subgoal: one of a set of goals that, when achieved, suffices to assure that another goal is also achieved. synonymous with *subproblem.*

subproblem: synonymous with *subgoal.*

subroutine (SUB)

(1) a sequenced set of statements that may be used in one or more computer programs and at one or more points in a computer program.

(2) a routine that can be part of another routine.

(3) in PL/1, a procedure that is invoked by a CALL statement or CALL option. A subroutine cannot return a value to the invoking block, but it can alter the value of variables. see *closed subroutine; open subroutine.*

suffix notation: synonymous with *postfix notation.*

supervisor: synonymous with *supervisory program.*

supervisory control: characters or signals which automatically actuate equipment or indicators at a remote terminal.

supervisory-controlled robot: a robot incorporating a hierarchical control scheme, whereby a device having sensors, actuators, and a computer, and capable of autonomous decision making and control over short periods and restricted conditions, is remotely monitored and intermittently operated, either directly or after reprogramming by a person.

supervisory program: a computer program—usually part of an operating system—that controls the execution of other computer programs and regulates the flow of work in a data processing system. synonymous with *executive program; supervisor.*

supination: the orientation or motion toward a position with the front, or unprotected side, facing up or exposed.

support environment: facilities (associated with an expert system-building tool) for aiding the user to interact with the expert system, including sophisticated debugging aids, friendly editing programs, and advanced graphic devices.

support facilities: see *support environment.*

surface knowledge: synonymous with *experiential knowledge.*

SW

    (1) see *software.*

    (2) see *switch.*

swap: in systems with time sharing, to write the main storage image of a job to auxiliary storage, and to read the image of another job into main storage.

SWCH: see *switch.*

swing: rotation about the centerline of a robot.

switch (S) (SW) (SWCH)

    (1) in a computer program, a parameter that controls branching, and which is bound prior to the branch point being reached. synonymous with *switch point.*

    (2) a device or programming technique for making a selection such as a toggle or a conditional jump.

switch control: the control of a device by a person through movement of a switch to one, two, or a small number of positions. The device used for such control.

switch core: a core in which the magnetic material generally has a high residual flux density and a high ratio of residual to saturated flux density, with a threshold value of magnetizing force below which switching does not occur.

switch indicator: synonymous with *flag.*

switching elements: synonymous with *logic elements.*

switch point: synonymous with *switch.*

SY: see *system.*

SYM: see *system.*

symbol: an arbitrary sign for representing objects, concepts, operations, relationships, or qualities.

symbolic address: an address expressed in a form convenient for computer programming.

178

symbolic atom: a data type permitting only the primitive operations of assignment and testing for equality. Two symbolic atoms are considered equal if they have the same print name, which is a sequence of alphabetic and special characters used for specifying the identity of the atom.

symbolic control: pertaining to control by communication of discrete alphanumeric or pictorial symbols that are not physically isomorphic with the variables being controlled (usually by a human operator). A device for effecting such control. cf. *analog control.*

symbolic expression: see *S-expression.*

symbolic inference: the process by which lines of reasoning are formed; for example, syllogisms and other common ways of reasoning step by step from premises. In the real world, knowledge and data—premises—are often inexact. Thus, some inference procedures can use degrees of uncertainty in their inference making. In an expert system, the inference subsystem works with the knowledge in the knowledge base. The inference subsystem in an expert system is one of three subsystems necessary to achieve expert performance; the other two subsystems are the knowledge base management subsystem and the human interface subsystem. see also *expert system; knowledge base management system.*

symbolic language: a programming language whose instructions are expressed in symbols convenient to humans rather than in machine language.

symbolic program: a program written in a language using mnemonic codes, in which names, characteristics of instructions, or other symbols convenient to the programmer are used in place of the numeric codes of the machine.

symbolic reasoning: problem solving based on the application of strategies and heuristics for manipulating symbols representing problem concepts.

symbolic representation: representation of concrete objects by abstract forms.

symbolic versus numeric programming: a contrast between the two primary uses of computers. Data reduction, data base management, and word processing are examples of conventional or numerical programming. Knowledge systems depend on symbolic programming to

179

manipulate strings of symbols with logical rather than numerical operators.

symbol-manipulation language: a computer language created entirely for representing and manipulating complex concepts (e.g., LISP, PROLOG).

synchro: a shaft encoder based on differential inductive coupling between an energized rotor coil and field coils positioned at different shaft angles.

synchronous computer: a computer in which each event (or the performance of any basic operation) is constrained to start on signals from a clock and, usually, to keep in step with them. cf. *asynchronous computer.*

synchronous data link control (SDLC):   a bit-oriented method for managing the flow of information within a data communications link.

syntactic: the formal pattern of an expression. cf. *semantic.*

syntax

(1)   the relationship among characters or group of characters, independent of their meanings or the manner of their interpretation and use.

(2)   the structure of expressions in a language.

(3)   the rules governing the structure of a language.

(4)   the relationships among symbols.

synthetic address: synonymous with *generated address.*

SYS: see *system.*

SYST: see *system.*

system (SY) (SYM) (SYS) (SYST)

(1)   a collection of people, machines, and methods organized to accomplish a set of specific functions.

(2)   an assembly of components united by some form of regulated interaction to form an organized whole.

system development: the fourth phase in knowledge engineering; consists of adding the great majority of knowledge to the system. For other phases see *knowledge engineering.*

T

tachometer: a rotational velocity sensor.

tactile: perceived by the touch, or having the sense of touch.

tactile sensor: a sensor that makes physical contact with an object in order to sense it; includes touch sensors, tactile arrays, force sensors, and torque sensors. Tactile sensors are constructed from microswitches, strain gauges, or pressure-sensitive conductive elastomers.

tag: one or more characters, attached to a set of data, that contains information about the set, including its identification.

tape row: that portion of a tape, on a line perpendicular to the reference edge, on which all binary characters may be either recorded or sensed simultaneously. synonymous with *frame.*

target language: a language into which statements are translated. synonymous with *object language.*

target program: a computer program in a target language that has been translated from a source language. synonymous with *object program.* cf. *source program.*

task: in backward chaining, synonymous with *goal.* Otherwise, synonymous with *context.*

task analysis: the second phase in knowledge engineering; requires the study of the target task that is presently performed, meeting with existing experts, and developing criteria that determine if the resulting system is successful. How the new system would best fit in the environment, where it will be employed, and the exact nature and quantity of knowledge that is to be captured in the expert system are all factors to be reviewed. For other phases see *knowledge engineering.*

task domain: in expert systems, synonymous with *domain.*

task-oriented language: a programming language that describes what the effect of robot action should be. cf. *manipulator-oriented language.*

task program: a program written by the robot user specifying the trajectory that the robot should move along in order to accomplish a given task.

TCP: see *tool center point.*

TCS: see *tool coordinate system.*

teach: to guide a manipulator arm through a series of points, or in a motion pattern, as a basis for subsequent automatic action by the manipulator.

teaching interface: the physical configuration of the machine or the units by which a human operator teaches a device.

teach pendant: a hand-held control box with which a robot can be moved and manually programmed.

technology transfer: in expert systems, the process by which knowledge engineers turn over an expert system to a user group.

TEIRESIAS: an experimental system for aiding human experts in formulating rules for rule-based expert systems.

teleoperator: industrial manipulators that are operated by a person in the control loop on a real-time basis. A person is retained in the system to control the process.

template matching: the pixel-by-pixel comparison of an image of a sample object with the image of a reference object, usually for purposes of identification, but also applicable to inspection.

temporal redundancy: the tendency of production systems to make relatively few changes to data memory (and therefore to the conflict set) from one recognize-act cycle to the next.

tens complement: the radix complement in the decimal numeration system. synonymous with *complement-on-ten.*

tera (T):   ten to the twelfth power; 1,000,000,000,000 in decimal notation. When referring to storage capacity, two to the fortieth power; 1,099,511,627,776 in decimal notation.

term: the smallest part of an expression that can be assigned a value.

ternary

(1)   pertaining to a selection, choice, or condition that has three possible different values or states.

(2)   pertaining to a fixed-radix numeration system having a radix of three.

ternary incremental representation: incremental representation in which the value of an increment is rounded to one of three values: plus or minus one quantum, or zero.

thin-film memory: a main memory unit using a thin film of metal as its storage medium. Information is stored by magnetizing the thin-film material.

three-bit byte: synonymous with *triplet.*

three-input adder: synonymous with *full adder.*

three-plus-one address instruction: an instruction that contains three address parts, the plus-one address being that of the instruction that is to be executed next, unless otherwise specified.

threshold

(1) a logic operator having the property that if P is a statement, Q is a statement, R is a statement, . . . then the threshold of $P, Q, R, . . .$ is true if at least N statements are true, false if less than N statements are true, where N is a specified nonnegative integer called the threshold condition.

(2) the threshold condition as in (1). see *threshold function.*

threshold function: a two-valued switching function of one or more not necessarily boolean arguments that take the value one if a specified mathematical function of the arguments exceeds a given threshold value, and zero otherwise.

thresholding: the process of quantizing pixel brightness to a small number of different levels (usually two), resulting in binary image. A threshold is a level of brightness at which the quantized image brightness changes.

throughput: a measure of the amount of work performed by a computer system over a given period of time; for example, jobs per day.

time constant: in an RC circuit, the product of R (ohms) and C (fards) expressed in seconds; that is, the time needed for an uncharged capacitor to charge to 63.2 percent of the applied voltage.

time tag: a number attached to a working memory element, varying monotonically with time and used for indexing the recency of the element.

TIMM: an inductive expert system-building tool, written in FORTAN and focused entirely on induction. With a nice prompted entry interface it is easy to develop a rule base. One unique feature enables it to identify the rule that is the closest match to existing rules within a particular knowledge base. Therefore, TIMM is used by those who have knowledge that either involves lots of similar rules with lots of possible outcomes, or situations in which the expert identifies a large number of variables that will effect a variety of outcomes, but lacks the ability to identify specific rules.

toggle: synonymous with *flip-flop.*

token

(1) an instance of a type.

(2) a unique atom used as a label.

(3) a symbol in the Rete match algorithm representing a working memory element.

tool: see *tools.*

tool builder: an individual who designs and builds the expert system-building tool.

tool center point (TCP): The robot arm is a means of moving the TCP from one programmed point to another in space. The control directs the movement of the TCP in terms of direction speed and acceleration along a defined path between consecutive points. During the automatic mode of operation, the position of the TCP and the orientation of the end effector relative to the TCP are known at all times by the control system.

tool coordinate system (TCS): the tool locations expressed in coordinates relative to a frame attached to the tool itself.

tools: computer software packages that simplify the effort involved in building an expert system; contain an inference engine and various user interface and knowledge acquisition aids, and lack of knowledge base.

top-down programming: the design and coding of computer programs using a hierarchical structure in which related functions are performed at each level of the structure. synonymous with *stepwise refinement.*

total systems: a strategy that places critical operational components of an organization under the complete or partial control of computers. synonymous with *integrated system.*

touch sensors: sensors used to obtain information associated with the contact between the finger(s) of a manipulator hand and objects in the workspace. They are lighter than the hand and are sensitive to forces smaller than those sensed by the wrist and contact sensors.

toy problem: an artificial problem, such as a game, or an unrealistic adaptation of a complex problem.

trace program: a computer program that performs a check on another computer program by exhibiting the sequence in which the instructions are executed and, usually, the results of executing the instructions.

tracing facility: a mechanism in a programming or knowledge engineering language that displays the rules or subroutines executed, including the values of variables utilized.

tracking

(1) in computer graphics, a technique of echoing a locator, using a cursor.

(2) the continuous position control response to a continuously changing input.

tracking, abort branches: see *abort branch.*

tracking, utility branch: see *utility branch.*

tracking window: in memory, the two limits in the tracking direction beyond which a robot will not attempt to reach. More than one tracking window can be defined for different segments of a tracking operation. These tracking window limits cause two separate types of action by the control—if the robot has just replayed a point, its control will check the position of the next point in the sequence; if the next point in a sequence is outside the tracking window, but away from it, the robot will move with the line until such time that the position of the TCP coincides with the tracking window limit.

trailing zero: in positional notation, a zero in a less significant digit place than the digit place of the least significant nonzero digit of a numeral.

trajectory: a curve in space through which the tool center point moves.

trajectory calculation approach: see *continuous-path control.*

trajectory planning: the determination of the actual trajectory along which the robot's end effector will move, subject to admissible velocity and acceleration constraints.

transaction file: a file containing transient (or relatively transient) data that, for a given application, is processed together with the appropriate master file. synonymous with *detail file.*

transducer: a device for converting energy from one form to another.

transfer units

(1) *bulk transfer units:* devices that transfer randomly placed parts such as a tote bin.

(2) *orientation transfer units:* devices that hold the workpiece in transfer devices (e.g., conveyor belts, chutes, guides).

transformation: the mathematical conversion system used in robotics to give industrial robots line tracking ability.

transient: pertaining to a program that does not reside in main storage, or to a temporary storage area for such programs.

transistor-transistor logic (TTL): a common electronic logic configuration used in integrated circuits characterized by high speed and noise immunity. synonymous with *bipolar logic.*

transparency: in expert systems, meaning "trust me," suggesting that its solutions are at least as good as those provided by human experts.

tree structure: a means of organizing information as a connected graph where every node can branch into other nodes deeper in the structure.

triple length register: three registers that function as a single register. synonymous with *triple register.*

triple-precision: pertaining to the use of three computer words to represent a number in accordance with the required precision.

triple register: synonymous with *triple length register.*

triplet: a byte composed of three binary elements. synonymous with *three-bit byte.*

true complement: synonymous with *radix complement.*

truncate

(1) to terminate a computational process in accordance with some rule; for example, to end the evaluation of a power series at a specified term.

(2) to remove the beginning or ending elements of a string.

truth maintenance: synonymous with *reason maintenance.*

truth table

(1) an operation table for a logic operation.

(2) a table that describes a logic function by listing all possible combinations of input values and indicating, for each combination, the true output values.

TTL: see *transistor-transistor logic.*

Turing test: a test whereby an experimenter asks questions and, based on the responses, determines whether the respondent is a human or a machine.

two-input node: nodes in the Rete match algorithm network that merge the matches for a condition element with the matches for all preceding condition elements.

two-out-of-five code

(1) a binary coded decimal notation in which each decimal digit is represented by a binary numeral consisting of five bits, of which two are of one kind, conventionally ones, and three are of the other kind, con-

ventionally zeros. The usual weights are 0-1-2-3-6, except for the representation of zero which is then 01100.

(2) a positional notation in which each decimal digit is represented by five binary digits of which two are one kind (e.g., ones) and three are the other kind (e.g., zeros).

two-plus-one address instruction: an instruction that contains three address parts, the plus-one address being that part of the instruction that is to be executed next unless otherwise specified.

type declaration: in computer languages, the assignment of identifiers to data constructs such as integers, real numbers, arrays, and strings. LISP is a weakly typed language where functions recognize the data objects for arguments.

U

uncertainty: with expert systems, a value that cannot be determined during a consultation. Most expert systems can accommodate uncertainty by allowing a user to indicate if he or she does not know the answer.

undershoot: the degree to which a system response to a step change falls short of a desired value, in reference to input.

uniprocessing (UP): sequential execution of instructions by a processing unit; independent use of a processing unit in a multiprocessing system.

unit: synonymous with *frame.*

UNIX: in software, an operating system developed by AT&T; a collection of many programs providing commands, editors, file managers, formatters, and programming languages.

unpacked decimal: representation of a decimal value by a single digit in one byte; for example, the decimal value 23 is represented by xxxx0010 xxxx0011, where xxxx in each case represents a zone. cf. *packed decimal.*

unstable state: in a trigger circuit, a state in which the circuit remains for a finite period of time at the end of which it returns to a stable state without the application of a pulse.

unstratified language: a language that can be used as its own metalanguage; for example, most natural languages. cf. *stratified language.*

unsupervised learning: synonymous with *learning from observation.*

unwind: to state explicitly and in full, without the use of modifiers, all the instructions that are involved in the execution of a loop.

UP: see *uniprocessing.*

upper arm: the portion of a robot's jointed arm that is connected to the shoulder.

urnary operator: an arithmetic operator having only one term. The urnary operators that can be used in absolute, relocatable, and arithmetic expressions are positive (+) and negative (−).

user: in expert systems, a user utilizing such a system, such as an end-user, domain expert, knowledge engineer, tool builder, or clerical staff member.

user-defined: program units that extend an implementation language.

user interface: see *interface.*

utility branch: a function used when it is necessary for the robot to take some form of corrective action in response to a signal that indicates the occurrence of some malfunction of the peripheral equipment. The utility branch is initiated by an external signal from the peripheral equipment rather than by an internal signal from the control.

utility program:

(1) a computer program that generally supports the processes of a computer; for instance, a diagnostic program, a trace program, a sort program. synonymous with *service program.*

(2) a program designed to perform an everyday task such as copying data from one storage device to another.

V

VA: see *virtual address.*

VAL: a manipulator-oriented programming language for robot programming. see also *WAVE.*

value: a quantity or quality that can be used to describe an attribute; for example, considering the attribute "color"—the possible values of color are all of the names of colors that we might use. If we are considering a specific object, we observe it and assign a specific value to the attribute by saying, for example, "that paint is colored bright blue."

value cell: in relation to a LISP symbol, contains the value that is bound to the symbol.

value set of a descriptor: synonymous with *domain of a descriptor.*

VAR: see *variable.*

variable (VAR)

(1) in computer programming, a character or group of characters that refers to a value and, in the execution of a computer program, corresponds to an address.

(2) a quantity that can assume any of a given set of values.

(3) in COBOL, a data item whose value may be changed during execution of the object program.

(4) in FORTRAN, a data item that is not an array or array element, identified by a symbolic name.

variable binding: in LISP, when a value for the variable is placed in the property list of the atom representing the variable.

variable-point representation: a positional representation in which the position of the radix point is explicitly indicated by a special character at that position. cf. *floating-point representation.*

VAX: a line of powerful computers.

vector attribute: an attribute that assumes a sequence of atomic values.

Veitch diagram: a means of representing boolean functions in which

191

the number of variables determines the number of squares in the diagram; the number of squares needed is the number of possible states (i.e., two raised to a power determined by the number of variables). see also *Venn diagram*.

Venn diagram: a diagram in which sets are represented by regions drawn on a surface. see also *Veitch diagram*.

verify: to check, usually by automatic means, one typing or recording of data against another; to minimize the number of human errors in the data transcription.

version space (of a concept): the set of alternative plausible concept descriptions that are consistent with the training data, knowledge, and assumptions of the concept learner. The set defines a partially learned concept and can be represented in terms of its maximally general and maximally specific members. see *concept description; partially learned concept*.

vertical stroke: the amount of vertical motion of the robot arm from one elevation to the other.

vertical tabulation character (VT) (VTAB): a format effector that causes the print or display position to move to the corresponding position on the next of a series of predetermined lines.

very large scale integration: see *VLSI*.

V format: a data set format in which logical records are of varying length and include a length indicator, and in which V format logical records may be blocked, with each block containing a block length indicator.

videcon (vidicon): an electron tube device used in a television camera to convert an optical image into an electrical signal through the scanning of an electron beam over a photosensitive window.

video display terminal: synonymous with *cathode-ray tube*.

virtual address (VA): the address of a notational storage location in virtual storage.

virtual image: in computer graphics, the complete visual representation of an encoded image that could be displayed if a display surface of sufficient size were available.

virtual machine (VM): a functional simulation of a computer and its associated devices.

virtual storage (VS): the notion of storage space that may be regarded as addressable main storage by the user of a computer system in which virtual addresses are mapped into real addresses. The size of virtual storage is limited by the addressing scheme of the computer system and the amount of auxiliary storage available, but not by the actual number of main storage locations.

virtual storage access method (VSAM): an access method for direct or sequential processing of fixed- and variable-length records on direct access devices. The records in a VSAM data set or file can be organized in logical sequence by a key field (key sequence), in the physical sequence in which they are written on the data set or file (entry sequence), or by relative record number.

virtual storage management (VSM): routines that allocate address spaces and virtual storage areas within address spaces, and keep a record of free and allocated storage within each address space.

virtual telecommunications access method (VTAM): a set of programs that control communication between terminals and application programs running under VSE, OS/VS1, and OS/VS2.

virtual unit address: in a mass storage system (MSS), an address for a virtual drive. The virtual unit address is assigned to any staging drive group. Each staging drive may have more than one virtual unit address, but only one real address.

visa point: the point through which the robot's tool should pass without stopping, when it is programmed to move beyond obstacles or to bring the arm into a lower-inertia posture for part of the motion.

VISICALC: the first of the electronic worksheet personal computer software products.

vision optical system: a device (such as a camera) which is designed, constructed and installed to detect intrusion by a person into the robot restricted work envelope, and which could also serve to restrict a robot work envelope.

vision sensors: sensors that identify the shape, location, orientation, or dimensions of an object through visual feedback (such as a television camera).

VLSI: Very Large Scale Integration. Pertaining to transistors and other electronic components on microelectronic chips. Chips in current production carry half a million transistors at most. American and Japanese firms are aiming for chips with ten million transistors on them.

VM: see *virtual machine.*

V-mode records: in COBOL, records of variable length, each of which is wholly contained within a block. Blocks may contain more than one record. Each record contains a record length field, and each block contains a block length field.

volatile memory: a memory system in a control system that requires a continual source of electric current to keep the data in storage.

VS: see *virtual storage.*

VSAM: see *virtual storage access method.*

VSM: see *virtual storage management.*

VT: see *vertical tabulation character.*

VTAB: see *vertical tabulation character.*

VTAM: see *virtual telecommunications access method.*

W

waiting time: synonymous with *latency*.

wait state: synonymous with *latency*.

walk-through programming: see *programming*.

WAVE: an early experimental robot programming language on which VAL was based, in part.

WD: see *word*.

weak methods: general techniques for problem solving in the absence of specific knowledge needed for more direct or efficient algorithmic solutions. see also *heuristic search; means-ends analysis*.

weight: in a positional representation, the factor by which the value represented by a character in the digit place is multiplied to obtain its additive contribution in the representation of a real number. synonymous with *significance*.

weighted value: the numerical value assigned to any single bit as a function of its position in the code word.

wide band: synonymous with *broadband*.

windows: sections found on computer terminals resulting from software used for dividing the screen into several different spaces.

window system: a system that divides a terminal's screen into segments, as when pieces of paper of various sizes are arranged on a desk.

word (WD)
(1) a character string or binary element string that is convenient for some purpose to consider as an entity.
(2) a character string or bit string considered as an entity.
(3) an ordered set of characters expressing information. (The term "word" may be prefixed by an adjective describing the nature of the characters, such as *binary* words.)
(4) in COBOL, a string of not more than 30 characters, chosen from the following: the letters A through Z, the digits 0 through 9, and the

hyphen (−). The hyphen may not appear as either the first or last character.

(5)   synonymous with *full word*.

word time: in a storage device that provides serial access to storage locations, the time interval between the appearance of corresponding parts of successive words.

work coordinates: the coordinate system referenced to the workpiece, jig, or fixture.

work envelope: synonymous with *working envelope*.

working area: synonymous with *working space*.

working envelope: the set of points representing the maximum extent or reach of the robot hand or working tool in all directions. The work envelope can be reduced or restricted by limiting devices which establish limits that will not be exceeded in the event of any foreseeable failure of the robot or its controls. The maximum distance which the robot can travel after the limit device is actuated will be considered the basis for defining the restricted (or reduced) work envelope. synonymous with *work envelope*.

working memory: synonymous with *short-term memory*.

working range: see *working envelope*.

working space (WS):   that portion of main storage that is used by a computer program to temporarily hold data. synonymous with *working area; working storage; working volume*.

working storage: synonymous with *working space*.

working volume: synonymous with *working space*.

work-in-process: products in various stages of completion throughout the production cycle, including raw material that has been released for initial processing, and finished products awaiting final inspection and acceptance for shipment to a customer.

work station

(1)   a configuration of input/output equipment at which an operator works.

(2)   a station at which an individual can send data to (or receive data from) a computer for the purpose of performing a job.

(3)   a manufacturing unit consisting of one or more numerically controlled machine tools serviced by a robot.

(4)   synonymous with *intelligent work station*.

work volume: the amount of space within which the robot can operate; includes the full range of points that can be reached by the robot's wrist.

world coordinates

(1) in computer graphics, device-independent coordinates used by an application program for specifying the location of display elements.

(2) a coordinate system referenced to the earth or the shop floor.

wraparound

(1) in computer graphics, the display at some point on the display space of the display elements whose coordinates lie outside of the display space.

(2) the continuation of an operation from the maximum addressable location in storage to the first addressable location.

(3) the continuation of register addresses from the highest register address to the lowest.

wrist: the manipulator arm joint to which a hand or end effector is attached.

wrist force sensors: sensors that measure the three components of force and three components of torque between the hand and the terminal link of the manipulator; consisting of a structure with some compliant sections and transducers that measure the compliant sections along three orthogonal axes as a result of the applied force and torque.

wrist movement: the ability to orient a gripper or any other end-of-arm tooling. *Pitch* refers to wrist movement in the vertical plane; *yaw* represents movement in the horizontal plane (swing); the ability to rotate is denoted by *roll*. see also *pitch; roll; yaw.*

WS: see *working space.*

X

XCON: an expert system developed to configure computers by specifying how all the components should be arranged and how they should be connected. synonymous with *R1*.

XSEL: an expert system for aiding computer salespeople.

XSITE: an expert system for ensuring that a site can handle the required power, air conditioning, and space for a computer installation.

yaw: an angular displacement (left or right) viewed from along the principal axis of a body having a top side, especially along its line of motion. see also *wrist movement.*

Z

zero-address instruction: an instruction that contains no address part, and which is used when the address is implicit or when no address is required.

zero-level address: synonymous with *immediate address.*

zero suppression: the elimination of nonsignificant zeros from a numeral. Zeros that have no significance include those to the left of the nonzero digits in the integral part of a numeral, and those to the right of the nonzero digits in the fractional part.

ZetaLISP: a very large dialect of LISP, with more than 9000 compiled functions available.